THE NOTEBOOK POEMS
1930–1934

Twenty Three.

The force that through the green fuse drives the flower
Drives my green age ; that blasts the roots of trees
Is my destroyer.
And I am dumb to tell the eaten rose
How at my sheet goes the same crooked worm,
And dumb to holla thunder to the skies
How at my clothes flies the same central
storm

The force that through the green fuse drives the flower
Drives my green age, that blasts the roots of trees
Is my destroyer.
And I am dumb to tell the crooked rose
My youth is bent by the same wintry fever.

The force that drives the water through the rocks
Drives my red blood ; that dries the mouthing
stream
Turns mine to wax.

Dylan Thomas

THE NOTEBOOK POEMS
1930–1934

Edited by

Professor Ralph Maud
Simon Fraser University, British Columbia

J. M. Dent & Sons Ltd
London

First published in this edition 1989

Copyright © 1965, 1966, 1967, 1988 by the Trustees for
the late Dylan Thomas

Introduction and Notes © Ralph Maud

This book is set in Photina
by Butler & Tanner Ltd, Frome and London

Printed and bound in Great Britain by Butler & Tanner Ltd
for
J. M. Dent & Sons Ltd, 91 Clapham High Street, London SW4 7TA

British Library Cataloguing in Publication Data

Thomas, Dylan, 1914–1953
The notebook poems 1930–1934
I. Title   II. Maud, Ralph
821'.912

ISBN 0–460–04792–5

Contents

Introduction

This volume brings together the poetry available to us for a consideration of Dylan Thomas's poetic development from the age of fifteen, when he began the first of the existing notebooks, to nineteen, when he was selecting from the notebooks the poems of his first volume, *18 Poems* (1934). In the same way that the *Collected Poems 1934–1953* (J. M. Dent 1988) is definitive for the poet's published volumes, the present volume, *The Notebook Poems 1930–1934*, is definitive for Thomas's preparatory poetry. A sample of Thomas's schoolboy verse is included, enough to indicate what skills the young rhymester had achieved in that line before he turned to free verse to release his authentic voice. Four of the 'innumerable exercise books full of poems', as Thomas described them to Geoffrey Grigson in 1933 (*Letters* p. 19), have survived, approximately two hundred poems in chronological sequence covering the period 1930–1934. These constitute the bulk of this edition. Thomas typed out his notebook poems when he was ready to submit them to publishers; about eighty of these early typescripts, some of which fill gaps in the notebooks, have found their way into the British Library and the Harry Ransom Humanities Research Center, Texas. In reply to Charles Fisher, who had asked him for a manuscript of a poem, Thomas wrote in a letter of early 1935:

> I write a poem on innumerable sheets of scrap paper, write it on both sides of the paper, often upside down and criss cross ways, unpunctuated, surrounded by drawings of lamp posts and boiled eggs, in a very dirty mess; bit by bit I copy out the slowly developing poem into an exercise book; and, when it is completed, I type it out. The scrap sheets I burn, for there are such a lot of them that they clutter up my room and get mixed in the beer and butter (*Letters* p. 182).

It is perhaps just as well that we cannot expect to find many sheets of these first drafts (a few extant odd remnants are included in this volume); the amount of apprenticeship poetry that we have is just manageable, and seems sufficient for the purpose of seeing how Thomas came to be the poet he was.

The notebooks also give insight into Thomas's development beyond *18 Poems*, as we see him returning to some of the early poems and rewriting them for publication, right up to his revision of "The hunchback in the park" (originally a May 1932 poem) in July 1941, within weeks of his sending the notebooks to London to be sold. Thomas wrote to Vernon Watkins on 13 November 1937 and enclosed "The spire cranes" (originally a notebook poem of January 1931): 'I've done another little poem: nothing at all important . . . I think it will be good for me to write some short poems, not bothering about them too much, between my long exhausters' (*Letters* p. 264). Thomas never revealed, at least in a letter, that "The spire cranes" and the other short poems he was sending to Watkins during those years were very early poems, and that his moving towards a 'new' clarity was really a recourse to old poems that happened to be clearer. However, in a letter of July 1938 to another correspondent, Henry Treece, he did not hide the fact that the so-called 'straight' poems of *Twenty-five Poems* were written before most of the poems in *18 Poems*, telling Treece that he intended to continue 'to shape into proper poems' for future publication 'the great deal of material still in mss books' (*Letters* p. 310).

It is useful to tabulate the sequence of Thomas's retrieval of the notebook poems that were subsequently published in his various volumes, though it is impossible to indicate here how much or how little revision was involved in each case.

18 Poems (1934)

August 1933 Notebook

"If I were tickled by the rub of love"	"Forty One" (30 April 1934)
"I see the boys of summer"	"Thirty Nine" (April 1934)
"Where once the waters of your face"	"Thirty Eight" (18 March 1934)
"Our eunuch dreams"	"Thirty Seven" (March 1934)
"A process in the weather of the heart"	"Thirty Five" (2 February 1934)
"I fellowed sleep"	"Thirty One" & "Twenty Two" (27 November & 5 October 1933)

"Light breaks where no sun shines"   "Thirty" (20 November 1933)
"When once the twilight locks"   "Twenty Nine" (11 November 1933)
"From love's first fever"   "Twenty Six" & "Twenty Four"
                                          (17 & 14 October 1933)
"The force that through the green   "Twenty Three" (12 October 1933)
   fuse"
"In the beginning"   "Fifteen" (18 September 1933)
"My hero bares his nerves"   "Thirteen" (17 September 1933)
"Before I knocked"   "Seven" (6 September 1933)

("Especially when the October wind" had an early version in typescript, and presumably came from the missing 1932 notebook. The other four poems included in *18 Poems* were written after the notebook ended in April 1934.)

Twenty-five Poems (1936)

August 1933 Notebook

"Foster the light"   "Thirty Six" (2 February 1934)
"This bread I break"   "Thirty Three" (24 December 1933)
"Grief thief of time"   "Eighteen" & "Five"
                                          (26 September & 26 August 1933)
"The seed-at-zero"   "Six" (29 August 1933)
"The hand that signed the paper"   "One" (17 August 1933)

February 1933 Notebook

"Shall gods be said"   "Fifty Two" (August 1933)
"Ears in the turrets hear"   "Forty Seven" (17 July 1933)
"Find meat on bones"   "Forty Six" (15 July 1933)
"Here in this spring"   "Forty Two" (9 July 1933)
"Why east wind chills"   "Thirty Seven" (1 July 1933)
"Incarnate devil"   "Thirty" (16 May 1933)
"And death shall have no dominion"   "Twenty Three" (April 1933)
"I have longed to move away"   "Fourteen" (1 March 1933)
"Was there a time"   "Five" (8 February 1933)

1930–1932 Notebook

"Out of the sighs"   "LVVVI" (7 June 1932) &
                                          unnumbered poem (1 July 1932)
"Today, this insect"   "II" (18 December 1930)

("Do you not father me" had an early version in typescript; other poems such as "Should lanterns shine" and "Then was my neophyte" could, it is conjectured, have had early versions in missing notebooks.)

The Map of Love (1939)

February 1933 Notebook

"The tombstone told"   "Thirty Six" (July 1933)
"We lying by seasand"   "Twenty Nine" (16 May 1933)
"Not from this anger"   "Twenty Five" (20 April 1933)
"O make me a mask"   "Eighteen" (31 March 1933)
"On no work of words"   "Eight" (16 February 1933)
"After the funeral"   "Six" (10 February 1933)

1930–1932 Notebook

"The spire cranes"   "IX" (27 January 1931)

1930 Notebook

"How shall my animal"   "42" (9 December 1930)

("When all my five and country senses" and "Once it was the colour of saying" were, it is conjectured, possibly revised from missing notebook poems.)

Deaths and Entrances (1946)

February 1933 Notebook

"On the Marriage of a Virgin"   "Sixteen" (22 March 1933)
"Holy Spring"   "Ten" (22 February 1933)

1930–1932 Notebook

"The hunchback in the park"   "LVVV" (9 May 1932)

In summary, thirteen of the *18 Poems* came from the latest notebook, as one might have expected. What one would not have expected is that approximately half the poems of *Twenty-five Poems* and *The Map of Love* had their origin in the notebooks. Even *Deaths and Entrances* has three poems derived from the notebooks. Only with these facts firmly in mind can one proceed to speak accurately about Thomas's middle period. It is a period of 'long exhausters', but very few of them; and in between are the more easeful poems that have been admired for their simplicity, but should be known for what they are – revised early poems.

These revelations about Thomas's poetic development gave force to the title of the first British edition of the notebook poems, *Poet in the Making* (J. M. Dent 1968). The present edition intends, likewise, to illustrate fully the role of the notebooks in the making of the poet, but it hopes to do so while being more inviting to the general reader. The previous edition, it now seems to me, had too much fidelity to the detailed idiosyncrasies of the notebooks. I was awed by the fact that the notebooks still existed at all, and felt that they should be presented with all their seams showing, all of the young Thomas's carelessnesses left intact. The present volume wishes to give the poems themselves a chance to be enjoyed – without misspellings preserved and footnoted, without square brackets indicating deleted words, without any intrusive paraphernalia. The emphasis has moved from the notebooks to the poems.

This is not meant to take away from, but to add to, the feeling of how remarkable it is to have these notebooks. A letter recently come to light makes it seem even more miraculous, for apparently Thomas left them all behind after staying at John and Clement Davenport's house in Marshfield, Wiltshire, and had to write for them, this in the middle of the Battle of Britain:

> In the pink bedroom we slept in and stored apples in and knocked about, you'll find unless they've moved a number of, I think, red small exercisebooks full of my old poems and stories. Would it be a lot of trouble for you to send them to me? I mean, will you? I've got a chance of selling all my mss, for about the price of two large Player's (*Letters* p. 479).

A week later, on receiving the notebooks safely, Thomas could write to Bertram Rota the bookseller, on 8 April 1941, that he was interested in selling them: 'I do not know, of course, if there would be a market for such work in bulk, as it were' (*Letters* p. 480). Rota turned to the only library which at that time had the reputation of being interested in the worksheets of living poets, the Lockwood Memorial Library of the University of Buffalo, New York. Amazing though it might strike us now, no one had ever asked the library for payment for manuscripts of this kind before. In fact, to discourage any deliberate manufacturing of worksheets, the librarian, Charles D. Abbott, had made it a rule never to pay. But he judged this case exceptional, and wrote to Rota that he had 'persuaded a private friend to buy them for us. It is a transaction which is most unlikely to occur again' (letter of 24 September 1941 at Buffalo). From Thomas B. Lockwood, the library's chief benefactor, came the funds to complete a sale the like of which will certainly not occur again. The four notebooks were bought for £6, £7.10, £6.10, and £5, respectively. They were accessioned by the library as *1930 Notebook, 1930–32 Notebook, February 1933 Notebook,* and *August 1933 Notebook.* They turned out to be school exercise-books without anything in them one would call notes; but these titles proved serviceable, and are now part of the language of Dylan Thomas studies.

When a reprinting of *Poet in the Making* was proposed by J. M. Dent in connection with the definitive edition of the *Collected Poems 1934–1953* it seemed a good opportunity to redo the volume. The fact that *Poet in the Making* has had a wide circulation over twenty years and will continue to be available in libraries has allowed for a certain latitude in the re-editing. Anyone who wants to know what words the young Thomas misspelled can consult the previous edition; here the misspellings are silently corrected, as are obvious punctuation errors. Words deleted in the notebooks are now not recorded in the text but in the notes. Where Thomas substituted words interlinearly, this edition either takes the later reading (and notes the deleted words only if they are interesting) or leaves the earlier reading in the poèm (recording the changed reading in the notes). The tendency has been in the case of the first two notebooks to accept Thomas's second thoughts, as they usually improve the poem. In the case of the second two notebooks, the original reading is usually preferred because it represents the integrity of the poem as first written. The result of these editorial decisions is a much more readable volume of poems.

A new feature of the present edition is the annotation of all the proper names, except the commonest, and of unusual words, where consultation with a dictionary might not, for one reason or another, suffice. The endnotes also contain pertinent biographical information and any indication of Thomas's own attitude to the poems, as found in his letters of the period. This specific, limited explanatory aid was the kind provided in the definitive *Collected Poems 1934–1953*; the notes in that volume can be consulted for the notebook poems that were eventually published in the *Collected*.

The present volume has been divided into seven sections, each with its own introduction. The four Buffalo notebooks still provide the solid core, of course; but enhancement comes from a preliminary section of selected early rhymed poems. Technically very accomplished and sometimes quite witty, they show where Thomas started from and why he had to turn to something else. In the free verse of the first two notebooks he forced himself to be himself; he shed the derivative. A section entitled non-committally "Typescript Poems" is placed where a missing notebook for 1932 would have been; it seems likely that these particular poems came from that period. Then we get the *February 1933 Notebook* and the *August 1933 Notebook*, with Thomas at a pitch of creativity not matched at any other time in his life. It is especially exciting to see well-known poems like "The force that through the green fuse" arising from these notebook pages in the context of a remarkably sustained output of very original poetry. The final section, "Collateral Poems", contains nine poems of varying dates that did not have a place in the other sections but, being of the period, deserve inclusion in a comprehensive picture of Thomas's early development as a poet.

In the Introduction to the first edition of the *Notebooks*, I expressed particular curiosity about a 'sudden leap' in the middle of the *1930–1932 Notebook*, where poems of automatic writing and drunkenness intrude, and a new very despairing note enters with "Through sober to the truth" (poem XXV, 3 July 1931) and with the general disgust of poem XXVI (28 July 1931):

> And whose affections aren't corrupt?–
> Listen and lie;
> The head's vacuity can breed no truth
> Out of its sensible tedium....

There I was ready to put this world-weariness down to the fact that Thomas had left school and had been forced to go to work. This explanation now strikes me as facile. I now believe that there occurred a deep revolution in Thomas's sensibility, however provoked. Youthful illusions were shattered, and the poet received a new knowledge of himself and his place in the world, to the extent that this period should be viewed as an accelerated or precocious maturing. The vision that was produced during this rite of passage was devastating:

> This pus runs deep.
> There's poison in your red wine, drinker,
> Which spreads down to the dregs

> Leaving a corrupted vein of colour,
> Sawdust beneath the skirts;
> On every hand the evil's positive....

This was written by Thomas on the day before his seventeenth birthday (poem XLIX, 26 October 1931). And then there is a period of six months with very few poems. And then poem LVVVI:

> Out of the sighs a little comes,
> But not of grief for I have vanquished that
> Before the agony. The spirit grows,
> Forgets, and cries.
> A little comes, is tasted and found good;
> All could not disappoint....

The tone of resignation felt in "Out of the sighs" was thought to indicate a movement towards maturity when the poem was published in *Twenty-five Poems* (1936) along with "Was there a time," "I have longed to move away," and a few other poems where a steadier voice seemed to have survived the wordy opaqueness of "I, in my intricate image." When, therefore, we are forced to recognize that these straight poems are actually early notebook poems the poet picked out for publication some years after their composition, then we can react in one of two ways. Either we confess that we were mistaken about the maturity exhibited and say that the wisdom in these early poems is spurious, or we can declare that Thomas went through an upheaval at sixteen, which, within a year, had led to poems of real maturity. I now tend towards the latter view.

There is striking confirmation in the case of "The hunchback in the park," first published in October 1941 and generally acknowledged to be one of the most satisfying poems of the *Collected Poems*. The notebook version, poem LVVV of 9 May 1932, is essentially the same poem. If there is maturity in the later published poem, it was certainly there in the seventeen-year-old's first draft.

I should like to offer two statements from authoritative sources, two people who knew Dylan Thomas well when he was seventeen, both of whom I myself met and admired. A. E. (Bert) Trick was the Swansea Labour Party man to whom Thomas dedicated "The hand that signed the paper," a canny man of the people. Trick wrote to me on 22 May 1962 in answer to questions about Thomas's political ideas in the period before he left Swansea:

His compassion and his intuitive concern for the underdog placed him on the side of the angels.... On reflection I would say that Dylan had a vague feeling for the Brotherhood of Man, an inclination to Pacifism, a deep abhorrence of violence, and as I have previously expressed it – a deep compassion.

Trevor Hughes was a valued early friend of Thomas's; he wrote a formal and sensitive statement for me when Buffalo library purchased his Thomas letters in 1961, including the following on Thomas at seventeen:

He showed the insight of a man in whom reading had become experience. He had no small talk. He was not sounding brass, a juggler with words. There was nothing spurious about him.... His apprehension was direct. His power was in and about him, and was always accessible to him.

Thomas's letters to Hughes, beginning in 1931, and to Pamela Hansford Johnson soon after that, are testimony enough in themselves. It seems to me that they reveal to any unprejudiced reader that Dylan Thomas was a remarkable young man, a genius who had matured by seventeen into the person he was destined to be. So the common complaint that Thomas failed to mature later in life is really meaningless. One doesn't have to grow up to be Joseph Conrad or Henry James in order to prove that one is mature. One doesn't necessarily have to fit a desirable profile. One matures into one's self, with a clear knowledge of one's place in the world. Thomas matured into himself, and he did it during the time of the notebooks. I find this an exciting proposition to take with me into a reappraisal of the individual notebook poems.

The acknowledgments made in *Poet in the Making* are applicable here; acknowledgment of more recent debts should be added. My chief debt is to Walford Davies of the University College of Wales, Aberystwyth, for assuring me that my help was needed as his collaborator on the definitive *Collected Poems 1934–1953*, which volume in turn led to the suggestion for a new edition of the notebooks. A subvention from the editor's home university, Simon Fraser University, Burnaby, British Columbia, helped to defray the cost of resetting the text. The project necessitated travel to review manuscript material at the State University of New York at Buffalo, the Harry Ransom Humanities Research Center at the University of Texas, and the British

Library, travel paid for by a grant from the Social Sciences and Humanities Research Council of Canada. Thanks are due to these three libraries for permission to print Dylan Thomas manuscripts in their holdings, and to David Higham Associates and the Dylan Thomas Trustees for copyright permissions. In the course of my recent travelling I was privileged to visit James Laughlin in Norfolk, Connecticut, a place-name imprinted on many of Dylan Thomas's American title pages. It is a pleasure to thank James Laughlin for information received in 1987 as well as for his guiding into print in 1967, with Robert M. MacGregor, the original New Directions edition of *The Notebooks of Dylan Thomas*. A final word of gratitude goes to Paul Ferris for a thoroughly reliable *Collected Letters of Dylan Thomas*; if it had not been there, the present volume would have had to wait for it.

Ralph Maud

Early Rhymed Verse

Of the 'innumerable exercise books full of poems' that Thomas mentioned to Geoffrey Grigson in 1933, only four survived. We have a good idea, however, of the kind of verse the others contained. The story "The Fight," in *Portrait of the Artist as a Young Dog* (1940), includes three poems from an 'exercise-book' of about June 1929. To those we can add a selection of what Thomas chose to publish in his school magazine. There are also a few poems from this early period available in library archives, poems copied out by hand, or typed for submission to periodicals. Finally, the four rhymed poems that Thomas deleted from the 1930 *Notebook* can be conveniently included in this section; they were clearly out of phase with the direction his poetry was about to take.

It was undoubtedly early rhymed verse that Thomas sent to Robert Graves when he was (he said) sixteen (he was probably a year younger). 'I wrote back', says Graves in *The Crowning Privilege* (1956), 'that they were irreproachable, but that he would eventually learn to dislike them'. Graves adds: 'Even experts would have been deceived by the virtuosity of Dylan Thomas's conventional, and wholly artificial, early poems' (pp. 132–133).

Juvenilia from Manuscripts

The Mishap

'I'll buy some powder! ram it down!'
Said little sonny.
'Apply a match, blow up the bees
And take their honey'.

Flash! the air is dark with bees,
And bits of sonny.
You could not bring wee sonny back
For love or money.

Ask of the breeze from foreign shores
Where sonny lingers?
North tells of nose, East speaks of toes,
West whispers fingers.

A piece of string, a twopenny knife
Well dipped in honey,
A button from his little vest,
That's all of sonny.

The moral:
Take warning.
The bees are in mourning.
Sonny's Pa cries, 'Alack,
Sonny's never come back'.

The Maniac

They say that the light of her eyes is gone,
That her voice is low, and her cheek is wan,
That her looks are sad, and strange, and wild,
Yet meek as the looks of a sinless child;

For the melting glance of her soft blue eye
Is chilled by cold insanity,
And the beauty that her bright form wore
Is the shrine of a living soul no more,

And her words discourse not music sent
From reason's governed instrument,
But, borne by her troubled fancies, stray
Like notes of the harp which the wild winds play.

I would not look on her altered brow,
Nor on her eye, so dim and soulless now;
I would not view her pale, pale cheek,
Nor hear her, in her madness, speak,

Nor see her smile, she knows not why,
While her tears flow down unmeaningly,
Nor her vacant gaze, the piteous token
Of a brain o'er-wrought, and a young heart broken.

No – on these things I would not look
For the brightest gift in fortune's book;
For she was joined with the fairest things
That rose in my youth's imaginings.

And oh! how oft have I turned away
From a brighter eye, and a cheek more gay,
That my soul might drink, to sweet excess,
The light of her pensive loveliness.

But her languid eye shall charm no more, –
Her smiles and her tears are nearly o'er;
For fond hopes lost and a heart o'er-laden
Have crushed, in her bloom, the guiltless maiden.

Song to a Child at Night-time

The moon is your lady; she sings you to sleep; the stars are
                              the dew on her hair;
Hushaby lullaby, lady of air.

The stars are your handmaids; they give you their love and the
                              delicate charm of their light;
Hushaby lullaby, lady of night.

So rest you and sleep you in the warmth of their care;
Hushaby lullaby, lady of air.

You hold the ilex by its stem

You hold the ilex by its stem
And touch its petals one by one;
You make them glad and tender them
With lifted fingers to the sun.

The flower will not join the sky;
It was the oracle that told
You how the stem and leaves should lie,
Stem close to white, and leaf to gold.

And now the sun denies it rest,
You will have tears to carry, bearer.

The ilex has a snowy breast;
There is not any flower fairer.

Verse from *Swansea Grammar School Magazine*

A Ballad of Salad

I cannot eat the red, red rose,
   I cannot eat the white;
In vain the long laburnum glows,
Vain the camelia's waxen snows,
   The lily's cream of light.

The lilac's clustered chalices
   Proffer their bounty sweet,
In vain; though very good for bees,
Man, with unstinted yearning, sees,
   Admires, but cannot eat.

Give me the lettuce that has cooled
   Its heart in the rich earth,
Till every joyous leaf is schooled
   To crisply crinkled mirth;

Give me the mustard and the cress,
   Whose glistening stalklets stand
As silver white as nymphs by night
   Upon the coral strand;

The winking radish round and red,
   That like a ruby shines;
And the first-blessing, onion shed
   Where'er your lowness dines;

The wayward tomato's glorious head,
   Cool cucumber sliced small;
And let the imperial beetroot spread
   Her crimson over all.

Though shrinking poets still prefer
   The common floral fashions,

With buds and blossoms hymn their Her,
These vegetable loves would stir
  A flint-heart's mineral passions.

Request to an Obliging Poet

Come, sing me a song of the succulent spring,
  Of the balmy and beautiful season,
Come, chirp me a chant of the peewit on wing,
  Or any fair fowl within reason,
Yes, lisp me a lyric of lilies and languor,
Of maids from Kidwelly and lasses from Bangor.

Come, pen me a poem of plentiful passion,
  Of fairies and flowers and fauns,
Come, scintillate sharply in Sitwellian fashion,
  Of parrots and perches and peacocks on lawns,
Yes, soothe me with songs of the serpentine sea,
Of naiads from Narberth and nymphs from Pwlldu.

Come, croon me a carol of sorrel and coral,
  Of mermaids and numerous moons,
Come, prattle a prologue with motive and moral,
  Of peaches and prisms and prunes,
Yes, warble away on Ophelia and Hamlet,
Of the gnomes from Llanllwch and the elves from Llansamlet.

In Borrowed Plumes

W. B. Yeats:

There was a pearl-pale moon that slid
Down oceans of ambrosial sky,
Under the drooping of the day's dusk-lid
Where darkness and her wine-waves lie,
And at that full nocturnal hour
She twined her splendid, curving hair,
And bent her body like a flower,

And glided through the evening air
Light as a cloud, and petal-fair.
She gained the garlanded and leaf-green mound
That tapered like a dove-grey hill,
To sink upon the deep grass without sound,
To press her face upon the lilting ground,
And twine her yellow hair like daffodil.
She raised fine, luscious fruit up to her lips,
Tasted the round grape in full-throated sips,
Smoothed upon her mouth the lovely pear,
When through the darkness coiled about the place,
The terror-scented darkness passion-dim,
A silver spider crawls, and weaves his web about her hair,
And weaves his silken rapture everywhere,
And looks into her wave-wild face,
And wonders why she weeps at him.

The Sincerest Form of Flattery

The sentimental sonnet:

I shall not come again, nor ever call
    The swan upon the waveless lake to me,
To see it sail, with no wing's sound at all,
    Along the waters of the mimic sea.

I shall not hear the singing birds again;
    The thrush's voice is, like a sweet ghost, gone
Out of the warmth into the bitter rain;
    There are no leaves for me to walk upon.

And I am tired of the too-hot sun
    Beating upon me till the night brings sleep;
There is no restfulness, the fierce day done;
    There is no quiet in the bright-mooned deep.

And by my side I hear the tropic sea
Lifting its voice like mine, but not to me.

The Callous Stars

The clear-eyed, callous stars look down
On darkened field and lighted town,
Slow moving through unmeasured space,
Or set in their appointed place,
From whence they shed impartial light
On sin and sorrow of the night,
Unstained, untouched by all they see,
Too bright and cold for sympathy.
We gaze upon the stars, and they
Behold us with a chilly ray,
In hard indifference to the sight
Of all we suffer in the night.
But could they feel as well as see,
The sky would droop from misery;
And hidden in a cloudy veil
The light of all the stars would fail.

Two Decorations

I

They come with their soft white hair
   In a power of candid motion;
Silver birds and flowers are there
   In their depths of the deep olive-ocean.
They gather the fruit of the grass,
   And the soil of the hills of the sea;
They will talk like high trees when they pass,
And carry wise beauty to me.

II

They do not approach my care
   In a filigree coming of death,
But move like a moon in the air,

9

Or shape a white cave of their breath.
And I cannot see their true pain
Carved in a dainty surprise,
Because of the wind and the rain
That blows like a cloud to their eyes.

Poems from the story, "The Fight"

Frivolous is my hate,
Singed with bestial remorse
Of unfulfilment of desired force,
And lust of tearing late;

Now could I raise
Her dead, dark body to my own
And hear the joyous rustle of her bone
And in her eyes see deathly blaze;

Now could I wake
To passion after death, and taste
The rapture of her hating, tear the waste
Of body. Break, her dead, dark body, break.

Warp

Like suns red from running tears,
Five suns in the glass,
Together, separate yet, yet separately round,
Red perhaps, but the glass is as pale as grass,
Glide, without sound.
In unity, five tears lid-awake, suns yet, but salt,
Five inscrutable spears in the head,
Each sun but an agony,
Twist perhaps, pain bled of hate,

Five into one, the one made of five into one, early
Suns distorted to late.
All of them now, madly and desolate,
Spun with the cloth of the five, run
Widely and foaming, wildly and desolate,
Shoot through and dive. One of the five is the sun.

The Grass Blade's Psalm

The frost has lain,
Frost that is dark with flowered slain,
    Fragilely strewn
With patches of illuminated moon,
    About my lonely head in flagged unlovely red.

The frost has spake,
Frost secretive and thrilled in silent flake,
    With unseen lips of blue
Glass in the glaze stars threw,
    Only to my ears, has spake in visionary tears.

The frost has known,
From scattered conclave by the few winds blown,
    That the lone genius in my roots,
Bare down there in a jungle of fruits,
    Has planted a green year, for praise, in the heart of my
                                upgrowing days.

The frost has filled
My heart with longing that the night's sleeve spilled,
    Frost of celestial vapour fraught,
Frost that the columns of unfallen snow have sought,
    With desire for the fields of space hovering about my single
                                place.

Rhymed Poems Deleted from the *1930 Notebook*

One has found a delicate power,
Quietly even and sound,
Under the wings of a flower
Raising its head from the ground,
A measure of ease and delight
In the sweet-footed dance of the night.

One has captured an image of joy,
Quietly even and mild,
In the clear-coloured eyes of a boy
Or the beautiful eyes of a child,
In the bird-like rhythm of night
Moving with ease and delight.

The shepherd blew upon his reed
A strange fragility of notes,
And all the birds and forests freed
The music of their golden throats.

He rose and walked across the grass;
His robe was trailing on the ground;
The birds and forests saw him pass,
And rose and followed without sound.

He led them over hill and glade;
They followed at his feet,
And listened to the sounds he made,
And all the sounds were sweet.

The Shepherd to his Lass

He said, 'You seem so lovely, Chloe,
Your pretty body and your hair
Are smoother than the rose and snowy,
Soft as a plum and light as air.

I give this garland for your head,
This little flower, and
I give you all I have', he said.
She smiled and took his hand.

The rod can lift its twining head
To maim or sting my arm,
But if it stings my body dead
I'll know I'm out of harm,
For death is friendly to the man
Who lets his own rod be
The saviour off the cross who can
Compel eternity.
I'd rather have the worm to feed
Upon my flesh and skin,
Than sit here wasting, while I bleed,
My aptitude for sin.

1930 Notebook

Thomas wrote "Mainly Free Verse Poems" as a heading to this note-book. He thoroughly crossed out the only four rhymed poems, and renumbered the rest in sequence. With these four poems relegated to the "Early Rhymed Verse" section above, the *1930 Notebook*, as presented here, is entirely free verse, forty-two poems, covering the period 27 April 1930 to 9 December 1930.

The general model for this free verse was Imagism. Daniel Jones, a daily companion of Thomas's at the time, has mentioned Richard Aldington and Sacheverell Sitwell as influences (ed. Tedlock p. 17). Writing on "Modern Poetry" in the *Swansea Grammar School Magazine* (December 1929), Thomas had singled out Aldington for 'accentuating the image and making it first in importance in the poem'; Sacheverell Sitwell was notable for his attractive obscurity: 'His difficulty is genuine, the strangeness of the picture he sees and wishes to explain, justifying the strangeness of the image he employs.' In a letter of 16 May 1938 Thomas tossed off the remark that his early poetry contained 'a lot of bits from whatever fashionable poetry – Imagism, Sitwells – I'd been reading lately' (*Letters* p. 297). The schoolboy essay on "Modern Poetry" had more gravity. Thomas held there that poetry was entering a transition period, reacting against the 'shrill crudity' of war poetry: 'Instead, we have a more contemplative confusion, a spiritual riot. No poet can find sure ground: he is hunting for it, with the whole earth perturbed and unsettled about him'. Written a few months before the *1930 Notebook* poems, this comment provides a perspective by which to view their tentativeness and self-absorption.

I

Osiris, Come to Isis

He stands at the steaming river's edge
With his soft arms in the air,
And snares the sun among his tangled hair,
And springs upon the wave's thick ledge,
And curls his arms around his hips,
Brushing the hot foam with his lips.
Slowly the river covers him,
The river of the webbed anemone,
The sadr on its leaf-green stem,
The river and the clouds' fair sea,
Until his feet are rested on the bed,
And top-turned plants are spinning on his head
Clutching his face with lean, long nails.

Osiris was the son of Seb and Nut,
A glacial god, a strongly-muscled boy,
Who, with one eye open and the other shut,
Caught tears and laughter with an equal joy.
He turned his hands and coiled his thighs,
Watery-handsome like a spotted stoat,
No parhelion in the Egypt skies,
But symbol of the sun's fierce throat
Steering its patriotic note   .
Out of the air's blue boat,
Among the corals and the sponges,
Wounding the water with his lunges,
So tortuous and dim,
Weaving a tribe over him
Of oval weeds with oval faces,
Symbol of the solace of the Nile,
Of the sun's grimaces,
And the moon's bright smile.

Osiris, Osiris, father of Horus,
Lost in the square houses,
Incarnated in a coal-black taurus,

17

Famous to the Alexandrian chorus
And Cotta's fine carouses,
You have exemplified the vicissitudinary, the odd
In fate and fortune,
And yet you were as pale as a lily,
You had no morbidity,
You had no abortion
Or limpidity,
Or bad birth-mark, or contortion,
You were a fair, and a strongly-muscled god.
Why were you born again in the belly of Apis
Like a bull
Out of reach of the body beautiful,
The firm breasts, and the kiss,
The intercourse and regret?

Under the lotus-earth perhaps
With happy stomach and fragrant chaps,
Judging the dead in their absence of vices,
Opening his eye and dreaming of Isis
Lying with Set or the bull, or both,
Side by side on the Nile's white cloth,
(Isis with beautiful breasts and mouth,
With a husband and child, or a cancer and growth)

He parts the water with his patterned knees
And hears the calm song of the waves,
The sadrs in their leaf-green graves,
The lilies and the hard-rock trees,
Moving their supple sounds along,
His hearing is so sweet and strong.
The harmony of grotto-water
Makes him desire Seb's fair daughter,
Earth and sky, with her sacred cow
Who gave her horns for the flat-haired brow.
She sits on a disced and symboled throne,
With a power of love through her skin
Like a sword in the flesh and a saw in the bone,

Fecund with sistrum and sin.

He makes a path with weeds and froth
Out of the river's white cloth,
Further and further down the Nile,
The sun her face, the moon her smile,
Until his body is a balm,
White and calm, white and calm,
Balanced on his shining arm,
Out of harm, out of harm.
He thought of Isis and her lotus-staff,
Pulling the water's wheel in half;
His legs are like her lotus-rod,
His breasts are feminine and white;
He is a happy but a virile god,
Seeking a bull-cow in the night
Under the waters of the Nile,
The sun her face, the moon her smile.

Osiris, Isis, you have made love
A mockery of love.
You have been thigh to thigh,
(Two eyes, one eye),
Breast to breast beneath its milk and heart,
But you have always been far apart.
Osiris, Isis, on the Nile's white cloth
You must unite in an Ishah growth,
And one mouth must not touch one mouth.
Apis must come to the cow
(Her horns are poised upon one brow,
While one hand holds the lotus-rod)
Or the cow to Apis
(Coal-black and beautiful,
A re-creating bull,
Half-in-half Serapis),
As the goddess must come to the God,
With her body clean for his.

He weaves the delightful waves with joy,

A glacial god, a strongly muscled boy,
Seeking perfection underneath
The river's hot, unwholesome breath,
Weeding the water with his knees,
Twining his body in anemones.

Osiris and Isis, dog-faced,
Even you can achieve beauty
From a sense of duty
And the wells of your straight bodies.

April 27ᵗʰ 1930

2

(Based upon themes from Mother Goose)

The lion-fruit goes from my thumb
And the branches stride from my hand,
Proud and hard. Now I may watch
The wings of the birds snap
Under the air which raises flowers
Over the walls of the brass town,
Near the sun with its dry stream,
Looking down on the turrets
And their gay windows, and their bars
Holding the princess back.
She is a lady of high degree,
Proud and hard, and she wears a coat
Clinging and strident,
Like a net or a basket for berries.
So I consider, I magnetize
With my sunshade up for the sun,
Soaking the sky and the cliffs
That return fury for fury,
My peacock chained to my wrist.

Beat the white sea thin,
Little miss,
Flatten the planted waves,
Plane them fiercely,

Be felt,
Mary, Mary, chop them with your garden-axe.

The boughs stand symbolic
In their stiff truculence
With folded hands folded piously,
Turning away from me,
Avoiding my eyes.
Their leaves shall not frolic
Or throw themselves into buildings
That grow above the traffic
And hold princesses back,
Who with gay coats surrender
Love to the postman or the clown.

Good leaves, where shall we wander
So that we may influence directly
In the fanfare of the sun?
The earth is good for nothing,
The lion fruit refuses,
And the branches shiver at my touch.

If you snatch the flashing snow,
Or the foam of the golden sea,
Or the forests from the brown soil,
You accomplish the great and the good
Like a god from the stars
Flying their angled flags,
Tom, Tom.
What is the body of a pig
Compared with the body of the earth
Which gives you water, and sweet fruits to eat,
Which loves you in return for a little love?

Hammer your verses
On the ground's dark crust,
Print them on the sky's white floor.

The princess from her turret watches,

Clad in her gay net coat,
Not to be refused, please names.

May 2ᵈ 1930

3

Poem Written on the Death
of a Very Dear Illusion

Grant me a period for recuperation,
I have lost my nearest relation,
Let there be tears.
My love is crucified
And split and bled,
Bruised and ravished by commercial travellers.
The lithe girls dance
With bright cloths glittering
And slippery breasts shining.
Oh, I have caused a disaster
Imitating an old master,
Rowing on the standing lakes,
So, I am tolerant,
I respect, I bow down,
My face bleeding in an affectionate smile.
I salute you,
I am a publican like yourself,
Hail, many-coloured Ceres,
I, too, gather and occasionally sow.
The dancing girls are arm-in-arm,
With beautiful thighs and ankles,
Oh, father, is there any harm?

May 2ᵈ 1930

4

You shall not despair
Because I have forsaken you
Or cast your love aside;
There is a greater love than mine
Which can comfort you
And touch you with softer hands.
I am no longer
Friendly and beautiful to you;
Your body cannot gladden me,
Nor the splendour of your dark hair,
But I do not humiliate you;
You shall be taken sweetly again
And soothed with slow tears;
You shall be loved enough.

May 6th 1930

5

My vitality overwhelms you,
My vigour is too heavy,
My love is a strong burden
That weighs upon your shoulders.
You bear my energy
With your slow fortitude,
Holding it up,
The muscles of your arms aching,
And your thighs burning with pressure.
So; you tolerate me;
I am to be tolerated;
Your love for me is lessened,
And has become the love of the animal,
The patient, intense affection of the cow,
The whining, respectful lust of the bitch.
Do not mistake me,
I do not ridicule the animal,

But your breasts and thighs and navel are not enough.
I want something more of you,
Something sexless and unmechanical:
The actions of love are stale,
Let me find a new medium,
A new method of intercourse.
Let me dispense with the animal:
The animal is not enough.

May 10ᵗʰ 1930

6

And so the New Love Came

And so the new love came at length
Healing and giving strength,
And made the pure love go.
She echoed my laughter
And placed my love upon her,
Bearing the voluptuous burden,
With the pure love coming after.
She led me onto the shore
Carefully by my hand,
Where the wild sea smoothed the sand
And polished the yellow grains.
She took me into the fields
When the moon had risen bitterly,
Into the place of rains
Treading the fine grass
With firm, elaborate feet,
And the old love follows our paths.
I gave my new love a kiss
And her lips were the reddest of berries
Which poison the mouth at a touch,
And her hair was a circle of snakes,
And her delicate eyes were seeds,
So my kiss became twisted

And bitter to my taste,
The new love hard and alive
Like a tree spreading its cruel roots.
'You are too strange,' I said
Into the pale shell of her ear,
'You bewilder me with your strength,
You hurt and do not reward.'
'I am Lilith,' she said,
And placed her savage mouth upon my neck,
And ran into the trees.

I went from the place of rains.

My new love brought me delight,
But my old love brings me her great faith.

May 17th 1930

7

On Watching Goldfish

You collect such strange shapes
In the cool palm of your hand,
You with long, sinewy limbs
And muscles breaking through the skin,
Such close sponges and water flowers,
Fishes, and green-scaled flies,
Each holding its synthetic perfume
Bottled and gay,
That it might sicken with its smell
Or blur at sight.
The fishes have an envy,
Like a bill through their fins,
To ascend, sail, parallel with the sky
In a motion of adventure.
You gather the pearls
From the sliding floor
For the necks of girls

To wear, this in the morning
But oh how different in the night.
The fishes in their floral beds,
The fishes in the white under-waves,
Over-bellying jocosely,
Limp and berry-eyed,
Their wet senses swimming faster
Than their clever fins,
The fishes on the sand
Waiting for the beachcomber,
Shy, open-mouthed, pin-teethed,
The fishes in the nets
Making the silly movements of swimming
Without hope or reason,
Bloodwet and beautiful,
How so wrinkled, stealing the fast perfume
From the sea's rose,
Tragedy, tragedy, tragedy, I repeat,
The sea is my enemy.
But there are still the gold-fish,
Slow and double their size,
Their scales are crisp,
They swim sedately because the bowl's palm is cool,
Feed them on seeds,
Change their water.

May 18ᵗʰ 1930

8

The lion, lapping the water,
Moistening his gums
And restoring his vitality,
Is a balanced creature
Who lives because he must,
And eats to live,
And takes, and fights, and loves
The lioness with a hard, bestial love;

His mind is clean
And he has no unnecessary vanity,
But he arouses a jealousy in me
Because of his strength and power
Which are unbreakable.
Even a lion in a cage
Is a vital, dominant creature,
With his vitality and dominance like a wall.
I cannot become anything but frail,
Ascetic, unbalanced,
My love cannot be anything but a poor return.
The lion and I
Accept the similar gift of death.

9

I Am Aware

I am aware of the rods
Of the high sun coming down,
Sharply, unwaveringly,
With bright tips to pierce,
Coming down pointed.

Where is the happy rain
That makes no enemies,
That does not cleave the grass
Or hurt the soil
Under its load of vegetation?
This is a harmful rain,
Harder than anything,
Which wounds the ground;
It does not cool as it should,
Ease the sinews of each plant,
Bring a well-oiled movement to each flower;
It pierces, pierces
Beneath the covering.

10

My river, even though it lifts
Ledges of waves high over your head,
Cannot wear your edge away,
Round it so smoothly,
Or rub your bright stone.
You stand a little apart,
Strong enough to tread on the sand
And leave a clear print,
Strong and beautiful enough
To thrust your arm into the earth
And leave a tunnel
Looking up at you.
The metallic rain
Cannot dent your flanks;
The wind cannot blunt
The blade of your long foot,
Nor can the snow
Smooth the prisms of your breasts.
Sea, do not flow
Against this side.

You stretch out your hands
To touch the hydrangeas,
Then take them away quickly
As the mouth of the tiger-lily
Closes about your clasped fingers
With uneven, spiral teeth.
Your hands are beautiful hands
With thin fingers
And milk-white nails.
Your eyes can be the eyes
Of the nightingale,
Or the eyes of the eagle
Rising on black wings.
Your voice can be the voice
Of the sea under the hard sun,
The sea speaking keenly,

Or the voice of the river
Moving in one direction,
In a pattern like a shell
Lying upon the yellow beach.
My river cannot rub your bright stone,
Which cuts into the strength
And takes the heat away.
My river has high waves,
But your stone is many-pointed,
And your side is steep.

II

The corn blows from side to side lightly,
Tenuous, yellow forest that it is,
And bears the steady wind on its head,
Brushing my two hands.
The flower, under the soil
Rounds its ungainly roots;
Blue flower,
In my continent of strange speech,
Divide and allow the path
Of my warm arm to touch you,
Then touch you again
Not with the drift of voluptuous fingers
But with the possession
That comes from obscure contact.
I must shape the corn
Into a phalanx that satisfies
The eye watching it move,
Mould and round and make mine;
Your tall, straight stalks
Inclining only to the heaviest wind,
Will be my architecture
And my pride above the flower
Whose roots I cannot feel;
I will mount you upon resolute love;

I will raise your columns.
Now flower,
Traveller through the earth,
Spiral and pleasant to the extent
Of your violent, blue way,
Shall I make more of you
Than the ghost from the grave?
Shall I turn you and better you
As I bettered the yellow corn
From one architecture to another?
You move in your island
Like a dark cloud high above the ground,
You circle your stalk
On the night sailing with care and skill.
I know your roots thrust fine, black teeth
Up into the soil,
And swell noiselessly.
In the spire of the top petal
Rings the loud bell of triumph,
As you arch and become longer.
My influence breaks your spell,
And now you can grow,
Now you can cut and hurt the cloud,
Giant-flower.

June 18th 1930

12

We will be conscious of our sanctity
That ripens as we develop
Our rods and substantial centres,
Our branches and holy leaves
On the edge beyond your reach;
We will remark upon the size
Our roots,
Beautiful roots
Because they are under the surface

Of our charm.
Give us the pleasure of regret;
Our tears sound wiser
Than our laughter at the air
Or the yellow linnet who does not merit it.
We will be conscious of our divinity
When the time comes,
Unashamed but not with delight,
Making our affections fast;
We will tie you down
To one sense of finality
Like a cave with one thread.
Under this shade
The kingfisher comes
And the fresh-water bird
With his pink beak,
But we do not concern ourselves,
Waiting, waiting,
Waiting for the bird who shall say,
'I have come to elevate you,
To saw through your roots
And let you float'.
Then will we rise
Upon broad wings
And go into the air,
Burrow our way upwards into the blue sky;
This shade
Has the dragonfly and the swordfish
Cleaving their own sedges,
The otter
Hand in hand with the mermaid
Creeping catlike under the water.
We will be conscious
Of a new country
Opening in the blind cloud over our heads;
We will be conscious of a great divinity
And a wide sanity.

June 6th

13

I have come to catch your voice,
Your constructed notes going out of the throat
With dry, mechanical gestures,
To catch the shaft
Although it is so straight and unbending;
Then, when I open my mouth,
The light will come in an unwavering line.
Then to catch night
Wading through her dark cave on ferocious wings.
Oh, eagle-mouthed,
I have come to pluck you,
And take away your exotic plumage,
Although your anger is not a slight thing,
Take you into my own place
Where the frost can never fall,
Nor the petals of any flower drop.

June 19th

14

My love is deep night
Caught from the tops of towers,
A pomp of delicious light
Snared under the tip of each stalk,
Dew balanced to perfection
On the grass delicate beyond water.
But beauty is a very old friend,
And in the coming and going of the seasons
It is lifted to a high pinnacle
So that we may admire it from a distance,
Not touching it with our cruel fingers
For they might break it into pieces.
We shall regret your delightful arms
Like two clouds,
And your delightful thighs

Like two towers,
Desiring the warmth they have once offered
But which we have once refused
More than the fine gift of sleep
Or the irretrievable gift of death;
We have need of you,
But we cannot touch you with our cruel fingers,
Or make your body a splendid place
For receiving us with more than a clasp of the hand,
More even than a gay laugh full of welcome,
More even than the pressing of your scented lips
On our white and hard skin.
Are we destined to become beautiful
Because we have admired but have not handled,
Allowing you your virginity in cool places,
And the heat of your own love
Where it cannot pierce or endure?
We are too beautiful to die;
All our life is bound to the green trees,
And in the cithern evening
The darkness is insistent,
Loading a pleasure of love upon us
In its great desire to overcome.

15

When your furious motion is steadied,
And your clamour is stopped,
And when the bright wheel of your turning voice is stilled,
Your step will remain about to fall.
So will your voice vibrate
And its edge cut the surface,
So, then, will the dark cloth of your hair
Flow uneasily behind you.

This ponderous flower,
Which leans one way,

Weighed strangely down upon you
Until you could bear it no longer
And bent under it,
While its violet shells broke and parted.
When you are gone
The scent of the great flower will stay,
Burning its sweet path clearer than before.
Press, press, and clasp steadily;
You shall not let go;
Chain the strong voice
And grip the inexorable song,
Or throw it, stone by stone,
Into the sky.

July 1 1930

16

No thought can trouble my unwholesome pose,
Nor make the stern shell of my spirit move.
You do not hurt, nor can your hand
Touch to remember and be sad.
I take you to myself, sweet pain,
And make you bitter with my cold,
My net that takes to break
The fibres, or the senses' thread.
No love can penetrate
The thick hide covering,
The strong, unturning crust that hides
The flower from the smell,
And does not show the fruit to taste;
No wave comb the sea,
And settle in the steady path.
Here is the thought that comes
Like a bird in its lightness,
On the sail of each slight wing
White with the rising water.
Come, you are to lose your freshness.

Will you drift into the net willingly,
Or shall I drag you down
Into my exotic composure?

July 17th

17

The hill of sea and sky is carried
High on the sounding wave,
To float, an island in its size,
And stem the waters of the sun
Which fall and fall.
Wind cannot spin the cloth
Of safety with such care,
Lacing the water and the air together;
Nor hail, nor season, weave
A hill like that.
Only the water loads its garden
With rich and airy soil,
Heaps on the paths the broken clouds,
And arches his long wave.
He is to plough the air,
Plough up and turn the sweet, blue fields,
And wrench the flowers by their roots;
He'll be at liberty
To plant what curious seeds he knows
When this is done.

July 20th

18

So I sink myself in the moment,
I let the fiery stream run.

How I vibrate, and the petunia too,
As, garden to your loving bird,
I'm all but cut by the scent's arc.
So in the sorrow after,
When you bird are flown away,
And the scent can please no more,
Your senses play the fool with me,
And, if you like, I ride
A knight upon a golden horse,
Or sit for you,
Or fly, or take the sea.

19

No, pigeon, I'm too wise;
No sky for me that carries
Its shining clouds for you;
Sky has not loved me much,
And if it did, who should I have
To wing my shoulders and my feet?
There's no way.
Ah, nightingale, my voice
Could never touch your spinning notes,
Nor be so clear.
I'm not secure enough
To tell what note I could reach if I tried,
But no high tree for me
With branches waiting for a singing bird,
And every nightingale a swan
Who sails on tides of leaves and sound.
I'm all for ground,
To touch what's to be touched,
To imitate myself mechanically,
Doing my little tricks of speech again
With all my usual care.
No bird for me:
He flies too high.

Aug: 8ᵗʰ

20

The cavern shelters me from harm;
I know no fear until the cavern goes;
Without his dark walls I die,
Without his winged roof
I have no place to cover me.
His noises, too, swing out like bells,
But when they stop, why, other sounds
Go on, sadder and more remote.
Seraph, you should come down.
That's no cavern in the air
To shelter round and round,
That's no river, either, to purify,
And each slight wave to bless the foot.
Cavern, my Jordan,
His silence is a silver charm,
Fine, bright stone.
Seraph, I wear my river round my neck,
My cavern's this and that,
But still it keeps me from the wind,
And does me good.

Aug 11^{*th*}

21

Woman on Tapestry

Her woven hands beckoned me,
And her eyes pierced their intense love into me,
And I drew closer to her
Until I felt the rhythm of her body
Like a living cloak over me.
I saw the cold, green trees,
Their silken branches unmoving,
Their delicate, silken leaves folded,
And the deep sky over them
With immeasurable sadness.

Her love for me is fierce and continual,

Strong, fresh, and overpowering.
My love for her is like the moving of a cloud
Serene and unbroken,
Or the motion of a flower
Stirring its pole stem in delight,
Or the graceful sound of laughter.
In the victory of her gladness
And the triumph of her pitiless gaiety
She became like a dancer or a pretty animal
Suave in her movements,
On the balance of her dark foot,
Stepping down.

She shall make for me
A sensitive confusion in the blood,
A rhythm I cannot break
Stroking the air and holding light.

And the roots of the trees climbed through the air
Touching the silver clouds,
Trailing their fingers on the hard edges
Pacing in kind praise.

I have made an image of her
With the power of my hands
And the cruelty of my subtle eyes,
So that she appears entertaining
Like the arms of a clean woman
Or the branches of a green tree.

Death comes to the beautiful.
He is a friend with fresh breath
And small, feminine shoulders,
And white, symmetrical lips
Drawing the energy from the love,
And the glitter from the fine teeth.

You shall comfort me
With your symmetrical devotion

And the web of your straight senses.
Your bitterness is masked with smiles,
And your sharp pity is unchangeable.
I can detect a tolerance,
A compassion springing from the deep body,
Which goes around me easily
Like the body of a girl.
So the ilex and the cypress
Mix their wild blood
With yours,
And thrill and breathe and move
Unhealthily with dry veins.

There will be a new bitterness
Binding me with pain,
And a clean surge of love moving.
In the fold of her arms
And the contact with her breasts
There will be a new life
Growing like a powerful root inside me.
The gestures of my love
Involve me in a gaiety,
Recall my old desire
Like a sweet, sensitive plant
In the barbed earth,
Holding a voluptuous clarity
Under the tent of its wings.

So the hills
Coiled into their bodies like snakes,
And the trees
Went away from the bright place.

28, 29 April 1929

22

Pillar breaks, and mast is cleft
Now that the temple's trumpeter
Has stopped (angel, you're proud),
And gallantly (water, you're strong—
You batter back my fleet),
Boat cannot go.

The raven's fallen and the magpie's still.
Silly to cage and then set free,
You loose, delicious will
That teaches me to wait,
Whose minute kindles more than the wise hour.
Temple should never have been filled
With ravens beating on the roof:
One day they had to fly,
And, there, what wings they had,
Poor, broken webs to strike the sky!
It was the magpie, after,
Bird on the mast (he contemplated),
Who flew himself because the boat remained
Unmoving in a shouldering sea,
Flew for a time in vain, to drop at last
And catch the uprising wave.

Pity is not enough:
Temple's broken and poor raven's dead;
Build from the ashes!
Boat's broken, too, and magpie's still;
Build, build again!

23

It's light that makes the intervals
Between the pyramids so large,
And shows them fair against the dark,

40

Light who compels
The yellow bird to show his colour.
Light, not so to me;
Let me change to blue,
Or throw a violet shadow when I will.
Today, if all my senses act,
I'll make your shape my own,
Grow into your delicate skin,
Feel your woman's breasts rise up like flowers
And pulse to open
Your wide smile for me.
Challenge my metamorphosis,
And I will break your spacing light.
Mock me,
And see your colour snap,
Glass to my hands endowed with double strength.
But if you break I suffer,
There'll be my bone to go:
Oh, let me destroy for once,
Rend the bright flesh away,
And twine the limbs around my hands.
I never break but feel the sudden pain,
The ache return.
I'll have to break in thought again,
Crush your sharp light,
And chip, in silence and in tears,
Your rock of sound.

24

Let me escape,
Be free (wind for my tree and water for my flower),
Live self for self,
And drown the gods in me,
Or crush their viper heads beneath my foot.
No space, no space, you say,
But you'll not keep me in

Although your cage is strong.
My strength shall sap your own;
I'll cut through your dark cloud
To see the sun myself,
Pale and decayed, an ugly growth.

25

Oh, dear, angelic time – go on.
I'll try to imitate your going,
And turn my wheel round, too,
As sure and swift as yours.
Between each revolution
(Wise time – go on,
My voice shall speed you
Though you need no strength
To make you turn, I know),
There's all my laughter smoke,
My grief a little empty sound,
And all my love a cloud
Who sails away from me.
I can't be happy.
Try today, try this time (sweet time),
Tomorrow's never.

26

And the ghost rose up to interrogate:
'When did you make the leopard yours,
Who was an animal but could not follow
The intricacies of another's path?
He follows now, smells you, and thinks,
A dolphin at a fountain's foot,
A sea-horse allegorically spouting
Water through his trembling nose.'

I hear the peacock shouting: 'Stop!
My high voice will never make you hear.
I stir my feathers to distract you;
The sound is louder than the sea's,
Steely and sharp and rich,
But still you move as steadily.
Oh, stay and let me speak,
For though my tears are bright
And my long tail is just the same,
I am a different bird, too sad
To make my colours cut.
My plumes, scythes for the night,
Who saved the earth alone
From drooping to the dark,
Are blunt. You do not understand.
March as you do,
Mechanically, with deliberate steps,
And there's an end to me.
I'll go, taking the rainbow with me.
The parrot and the dahlia'll take my hand.
Gillyflower, Gillyflower, you will come with me.
This is our way,
The bright and hundred-coloured stairs.'
The wheels revolve, wheel within wheel,
Shining and multiplex machines;
Their voice obliterates the bird's,
Weaker and wiser, touching the highest air.
Peacock's gone.
Run smoothly, run carefully,
Run smoothly, run carefully.
Keep rhythm, keep rhythm,
You shall break the herb and the tree
Under your glistening heel.
I reproach the hollow perfection,
And the rootless power.
I praise the grotesque,
The peacock and the gillyflower,
The dolphin and the mustard-bird.
The wheels go round and round.

27

When I allow myself to fly,
There is no sense of being free;
Only the other loosening me
Can send that voluminous delight,
And make the wind that hurries by
Keener to invigorate.
As you travel
My head shall follow your course,
Inclining as you incline.
No flower follows the ardent sun
More faithfully in every movement
Than I do at your garment's hem.
Unchain me, and I fly so high
I rest myself upon a cloud at will,
Sing with such pitiless technique
My tree bows down beneath the lyric weight,
The leaves drop down, a note on each.
You cannot shine forever,
And when your lustre vanishes,
I follow your uncertain ghost.
But can he set me free?
Could his hand break the chain?
His light could never make me see,
Trembling, white rod which goes
Around me.
And is an echo worth my constancy?

28

Admit the Sun

Admit the sun into your high nest
Where the eagle is a strong bird
And where the light comes cautiously
To find and then to strike;
Let the frost harden
And the shining rain
Drop onto your wings,
Bruising the tired feathers.

I build a fortress from a heap of flowers;
Wisdom is stored with the clove
And the head of the bright poppy.
I bury, I travel to find pride
In the age of Lady Frankincense
Lifting her smell over the city buildings.
Where is there greater love
For the muscular and the victorious
Than in the gull and the fierce eagle
Who do not break?

Take heed of strength!
It is a weapon that can turn back
From the well-made hand
Out of the air it strikes.

29

A Section of a Poem called
"Hassan's Journey into the World"

We sailed across the Arabian sea,
Restless to interrupt the season
And for our castles and unshaken trees
Take the bright minaret.

The world was tired, tide on tide
Falling below our boat
With slow deliberation,
And bearing its tiny water-lass
As if she were as big as we.
'If we are outcasts', Hassan said,
'Then what is she?'
Pointing to her who rode so easily.
The second clown began to laugh.
'Heigh-ho', he said, 'anchor my joy
At seeing everything so upside-down
Or it will turn and strike against
Whatever grief you hide'. His face
Was webbed in smiles; a foot
Of laughter spread upon the cheeks
That, cherry-red and touched with blue,
Quivered if any jest would spring
Out of the tall wave's murmuring.
But with the night none came
To close the door and step inside.
The second clown began to dream.
'Heigh ho', he thought, 'she comes to me;
Button my collar; is my monkey trim?
Have I my best bucolic bells
To tinkle in her tiny ears
And make her laugh?'
So, softly, like a lady
Stept off the sounding moon,
She walked across to sit beside
The poor old fool who lay asleep.
'Boy!' she sang. But his eyes
Were closed to catch the fullest light
That made the dream-world sweet,
Careless and light as water
Running down the chiming rocks,
Vapid as the rising night
Who comes but does not syncopate
With other birds and animals.
'I am the turtle', said the turtle,

'My shell contains a thousand things,
My little eyes can see a lot'.
'Boy!' The clown's goodnight
Was very hard to penetrate;
The turtle laid a velvet foot
Upon the old fool's mouth.
'Imitate; not syncopate;'
Who heard the turtle's voice?
'Your kiss is soft, my lady-moon,
Your velvet lips delight mine own,
Send the gay moisture of your breath
Into my lungs, and down and down.
You kiss my heart, and I am glad'.
But, no, the turtle is awake
To every spark that kindles love
With such a free activity,
Pure and incorporeal, a shell away
To leave the body pink and nice,
Untouched, unfalsified, a silver god
Who knows the wise flesh's wants.
The lady sang. Hassan said 'Lady', but she did not look
Where he stood smiling at the cabin door.
'One could not tarnish our love
By giving pain,
Or taking me away from you
And putting you to ridicule;
You are too worthy of my love
For anything or one to change it;
Believe in the wisdom of our love,
And we shall grow to hope for love
That gives and does not ask for anything'.
But Hassan had waited too long;
The lady was melting, was melting,
Her poor little feet and her hands
Turning quite slowly to water.
Love, like a stone, struck the jester.
His old face was firm and young,
His voice was clear:
'Goodbye, my Aegis, but remember,

This is not your last visit.
You shall bring your love again
For me to hide behind,
Secrete my shame, and lose my vanities'.
He seized her snowy hand to kiss.

30

I know this vicious minute's hour;
It is a sour motion in the blood,
That, like a tree, has roots in you,
And buds in you.
Each silver moment chimes in steps of sound,
And I, caught in mid-air perhaps,
Hear and am still the little bird.
You have offended, periodic heart;
You I shall drown unreasonably,
Leave you in me to be found
Darker than ever,
Too full with blood to let my love flow in.
Stop is unreal;
I want reality to hold within my palm,
Not, as a symbol, stone speaking or no,
But it, reality, whose voice I know
To be the circle not the stair of sound.
Go is my wish;
Then shall I go,
But in the light of going
Minutes are mine
I could devote to other things.
Stop has no minutes, but I go or die.

November 3ʳᵈ

31

Claudetta, You, and Me

Her voice is a clear line of light
Coming from the end of her world
Into the uneasy centre of mine,
And her hair is a forest whose trees
I have planted, in thought,
Time upon time.
Thus is the contact made,
The both flames rising come together,
And the tips of the fiery waves
Met lightly.
So shall we be comrades,
So shall we be lovers,
You in your clear serenity,
I in my trembling obscurity,
And the rose shall grow to be a tall flower,
And the rain of seasons change my colour,
Before the love I bear you break.
Elucidate what binds us now;
Follow the path of every curious thought
We think between us,
And then, lady for lord, the shy gazelle
Has eyes to pierce beneath your mind,
And velvet skin to feel.
You have looked for a goddess
And found a lorette;
You would have been her god,
But now you are only her leman,
While Claudetta and I pass over the golden fields,
And still the gazelle has eyes for you.

November 4ᵗʰ

32

Come, black-tressed Claudetta, home
To me, who, when you go,
Fall into melancholy.
You said 'The shepherd by the brook,
Singing to soothe his cares,
Befriended me, and told me how
The swallow was the bird he loved.
I love the quail'.
Living within her eyes, I saw with them
The swallow darting up,
And he, the shepherd,
Seeing it fly so splendidly,
Telling his cares his secret love for it.
I felt her eyes
Gazing at where the quail would be,
And knew I never could possess
Her love so truly.
She was the quail's.
Its wings would break if she would touch,
So that she loved it more
If that could be.
Claudetta, when your quail is near,
You rise yourself on wings.
Come, black-tressed Claudetta, home;
The shepherd loves;
You are the queen
I could not bear to see be his –
His swallow flies too high.
Quail, then, be mine.

November 5th 1930

33

Cool, oh no cool,
Sharp, oh no sharp,
The hillock of the thoughts you think
With that half-moulded mind I said was yours,
But cooler when I take it back,
And sharper if I break asunder
The icicle of each deliberate fancy.
For when I bought you for a thought (you cost no more),
How could I smooth that skin
Knowing a dream could darken it,
And, the string pulled, some mental doll
Ravage and break,
How kiss, when doll could say,
'Master, her mouth is sawdust
And her tongue, look, ash,
    Part from her,
    Part from her,
Sweet, automatic me knows best'?
But you shall not go from me, creation;
Oh no, my mind is your panopticon;
You shall not go unless I will it
And my thoughts flow so uneasily
There is no measured sea for them,
No place in which, wave perched on wave,
Such energy may gain
The sense it has to have.
You wish to stay my prisoner
Closed in your cell of secret thoughts,
And I, your captor, have my love to keep
From which you may not fly.

34

They brought you mandolins
On which you might make song,
And, plucking each string lightly,
Send what you dreamt into the sky.
I'll make your thoughts for you,
Catch them in bird-like notes,
On fountains of the brightest sound
Rising, oh rising, above your own fair head.

The dreamer asks my pity.
'My fancies are fallen', she whispers,
Her finger to her lips,
'Secretly fallen like snow come at night
Or the sweet, invisible rain
You told me of.
I planted my dreams with the myrtle tree,
For, when it would grow,
I wished my flowers, too,
Like myrtle foliage to which you sing
"Myrtle, good myrtle, velvet tree, wither;
The turtle is come for his revenge;
He will not have you slight him so".
I was a vain creature,
And a too proud lady.'
And wishing for patience
So that you might not wait so anxiously,
You stood at the gates
But I would not let you in.
Your face was a dark shadow
I could not penetrate,
And your voice was cool and low
Telling me what I already knew.
I was aware of the garden
Only by the curious smell of the lemon-flower
Coming into my room,
Not by sight or by touch.
'I should have chosen a common tree

To seed with my common dreams,
Feathery animals loving me much,
But no feather more affectionate
Than the other's dear fancies
I laughed at, not guessing
Beauty was beauty to that one.
I should have made
An armour to cover my dreams,
To fasten it then, sweeten it then,
And to liberate at last'.

Now is my rare voice bidden
To hymn the lady I love;
I think she is fairer than any;
I know I am glad when she comes.

35

The air you breathe encroaches
The throat is mine I know the neck
Wind is my enemy your hair shant stir
Under his strong impulsive kiss
The rainbow's foot is not more apt
To have the centaur lover
So steal her not O goat-legged wind
But leave but still adore
For if the gods would love
Theyd see with eyes like mine
But should not touch like I
Your sweet inducive thighs
And raven hair.

36

When all your tunes have caused
The pianola's roll to break,
And, no longer young but careful,
There are no words by which you might express
The thoughts you seem to let go by,
You might consider me.
I want no words to show
How many clever thoughts I have accumulated
With all the squirrel's shy avidity
(Best thoughts keep closest to the breast
And never see their concrete shapes;
Your bosom's sun has no equivalent);
You can express me
In wind, or snow, or wave, or sand.

37

Written in a classroom

Am I to understand
You say what I should comprehend,
And make the words I knew
By sight and hearing
Words to the whirling head?
Your voice recedes,
Goes up to circle and comes down to earth,
But leaves no tail
Of reason for my penetrated mind
To clutch and use
For doing what you might have asked.
Shaft of winter morning light
Is realler than your faces, boys,
And I preoccupy myself.
Am I to understand
That those high sounds you speak,

Hope, hope against anger, hope against hope,
Pity for, despair, or hate of, me
Who hopes not anger,
Should strike my brain to answer yes,
Or smile the comprehending smile?
Your voice recedes. It drowns my thoughts.
It touches them I see unreal
Beside the river of the flowing sun,
And then is drowned itself
Within the bird's outcry.
I loved her once,
Lived for her smile and died too many times,
Cried like a child
The more I knew
Love was a channel of delight
Clogged up with symbols of the tongue.
Love was a tiny boy.
Love was a light on you
Speaking your sounds,
And, after that, regret,
Sad night to hope,
Dark, dark despair she fathomed for me.
You speak, and I can hear
Her saying in your words,
'No. No. No. You mean
A voice, a smile to me.
How can I love a smile, my dear?'
Poor boy, she said,
And I preoccupy myself
Along with you.
Am I to understand
You say what I should comprehend?
Am I to understand, dear girl, dear girl?
This thought and that.
Face upon voice and voice on face.
Speak your bewildering sounds.

38

Hand in hand Orpheus
and Artemis go walking
into the void of sense
you stopped the eagle in its flight
you took Endymion to your place
now you go walking into sense
now you go walking into sense
and I am left to love your lies
and drown my thoughts
before I die of drowning.
So I place my hand upon my heart
the laugh clown laugh is all I have
roses and wine before I die
or cough my stomach up
the sweet sweet lie goes walking into sense
you sweet sweet trull
with drifting hair
and rotten breath gone
down the drain of sense
into the calculated sea.

39

I, poor romantic, held her heel
Upon the island of my palm,
And saw towards her tiny face
Going her glistening calves that minute.
There was a purpose in her pointed foot;
Her thighs and underclothes were sweet,
And drew my spiral breath
To circumambulate for decency
Their golden and their other colour.
The band was playing on the balcony.
One lady's hand was lifted,
But she did not cry, 'I see;

I see the man is mad with love'.
Her fan burst in a million lights
As that her heel was lifted,
Gone from my palm to leave it marked
With quite a kind of heart.
She is on dancing toes again,
Sparkling a twelve-legged body
And many arms to raise
Over her heel and me.
I, poor romantic, contemplate
The insect on this painted tree.
Which is the metal wing
And which the real?

22ᵈ November 1930

40

Oh! the children run towards the door,
Opening a thousand times before they blink,
And there are fifty Xmas trees
Showing the snow on every thirtieth branch
Outside the house, but not too far.
Clap hands! Clap hands! Father has cherries
And mother a violin;
There's food and there's music for all of them now,
And the Xmas trees for the picking.
The salamanders sit them down
And eye the children all the while,
As if to stop
Them thinking they would miss
The table and the penny candles.
The nymphs, however, cannot look
Into the room behind the blinds,
And those that live
In channels underneath the earth
Pierce all in vain
Their walls to clamber through.

Each glass its note,
A corner's sound,
Full for their throats,
And for their ears,
The cherry and the violin
That eat and play in one.
Drink, you've ten fingers;
Eat, there's your mouth;
Bed for you, children,
But not before the violin
Has made the wine-glass fall
Upon the unpierced earth in shame.
Darkness is best;
The mouse knows that;
So do the salamanders,
And they awake to draw the blinds
The nymphs are barriered by;
So, air and fire, amused from them,
Forget the mole
Snouting his dark hole all the time.

41

Tether the first thought if you will,
And take the second to yourself
Close for companion, and dissect it, too,
It stays for me
With your no toil.
With fingers moving you will see it stir,
And then the stolen third –
Now you have turned the nervous tap –
Flow into place.
 Why does the foremost wave await
 Until its follower arrives
 Before it pulses and begins
 To weave, swallow, careful leap?
But you must see my images

From exultation to despair,
Or formed from speech
That's formed by smoke in sleep,
Or moving in the thoughts you steal.
Hope is for you and love,
But what remains of them when I have done with them –
I lift to look, to see,
Ah, it is fair I more than glance at,
And, clever wish, I long to kill,
Or kill –
Is not for your regard.
Have I to show myself to you
In every way I am,
Classic, erotic, and obscene,
Dead and alive,
In sleep and out of sleep,
Tracking my sensibilities,
Gratifying my sensualities,
Taking my thoughts piece from piece?
Look down.
Look down.

42

How shall the animal
Whose way I trace
Into the dark recesses
Be durable
Under such weight as bows me down,
The bitter certainty of waste,
The knowing that I hatch a thought
To see it crushed
Beneath your foot, my bantering Philistine?

I build a tower and I pull it down;
The flying bird's a feather,

Has no flesh or bone,
Carried by any wind to anywhere.

My senses see.
Speak then, o body, shout aloud,
And break my only mind from chains
To go where ploughing's ended.
The dancing women all lie down;
Their turning wheels are still as death;
No hope can make them glad,
Lifting their cheery bodies as before
In many shapes and signs,
A cross of legs
That Christ was never nailed upon,
A sea of breasts,
A thousand sailing thighs.

How shall the animal,
Dancer with lightest heel,
High bird
Who goes
Straight in a wingèd line
Beyond the air,
Horse in the meadow
With the plough for toiling,
A boy to call,
And all the shining ground to tread,
Woman and sloe,
Still dance, fly, labour, be,
When sense says stop?
Purpose is gone;
I try to hold, but can't,
Compress, inflate, grow old,
With all the tackle of my certain magic
Stone hard to lift.

December 9th 1930

60

1930–1932 Notebook

As with the *1930 Notebook*, Thomas headed the first page of the *1930–1932 Notebook* with the comment: "Mainly Free Verse Poems." He later crossed it out, perhaps when the free flow of words had run its course, and he realized that the need to rhyme had begun to reassert itself. His general methodology in this notebook is revealed by advice he gave to his friend Trevor Hughes not to spend too much time polishing his writing:

> Why not, for a change, fire off round after round of ammunition from any old gun you can get hold of. You'll miss hundreds of times, but you're bound to get the bull's eye a lot of times, too. You'll find the hit-or-miss, the writing with no plot, technique will help you considerably in loosening your mind and in getting rid of those old stifling memories which may, unless you are careful, get in the way of your literary progress (*Letters* p. 14).

This was written in February 1933, but Thomas was describing his own experience during the period of the *1930–1932 Notebook*. There is no other time when he seems more to have exhibited this kind of wasteful virtue, to have obeyed his instinct to 'write, write, regardless of everything' (*Letters* p. 14).

Thomas signed the last page: 'End of Book July the Second 1932. This has taken a hell of a time'. He had begun the notebook as a bored schoolboy of sixteen, and finished it when he was seventeen-and-a-half, a frustrated newspaper employee. It was to be another year before any London periodical would accept a poem for publication. He was writing in isolation and without bounds, and finding it burdensome, at least until April 1932, when a change of mood occurred. In February 1932 he had predicted in a letter: 'Whatever talents I possess may suddenly diminish or may suddenly increase' (*Letters* p. 7). After that comment, there were no poems for two months; and then a remarkable blossoming.

I

This love – perhaps I overrate it,
And make my god an any woman
With lovely hair and teeth,
Praising an empty gesture as a world of meaning,
Thinking a smile meant faith,
And a word so lightly uttered
Immortality.
I am too gay perhaps,
Too solemn, insincere,
Drowned in too many thoughts,
Starved of a love I know
True and too beautiful.
But too much love, I know,
Will make me weak,
I spend my great strength so
In every motion
To your hand, or lip, or head.

Dec 1930

II

Today, this hour I breathe
In symbols, be they so light, of tongue and air,
The now I have space
And time that is already half
More than that I tell you in,
I have divided
Sense into sight and trust.
The certain is a fable.
Oh, iron bird, you are not credited
But fly, against joy, for that is not
If sea is rare
That does not imitate
Boy with the voice, or tympani,
The same, you likeable machine.

63

As well, creature has no flesh
And does not try the sun with seeing,
But measures his own length on a wall,
And leaves his shell
A butterfly before the chrysalis,
A flying egg of inhibition.
My she loves me is easy prey
For moving down another shaft,
Up to the hilt in going-backs,
And here, upon a hand,
A hundred years are by me cut.

Dec 18 1930

III

Sometimes the sky's too bright,
Or has too many clouds or birds,
And far away's too hot a sun
To nourish thinking of him.
Why is my hand too blunt
To cut in front of me
My horrid images for me,
Of over-fruitful smiles,
The weightless touching of the lip
I wish to know
I cannot lift, but can,
The creature with the angel's face
Who tells me hurt,
And sees my body go
Down into misery?
No stopping. Put the smile
Where tears have come to dry.
The angel's hurt is left;
His telling burns.
Sometimes a woman's heart has salt,
Or too much blood;
I tear her breast,

And see the blood is mine,
Flowing from her but mine,
And then I think
Perhaps the sky's too bright;
And watch my hand,
But do not follow it,
And feel the pain it gives,
But do not ache.

Dec 19 1930

IV

Here is the bright green sea,
And, underneath, a thousand fishes
Moving their scaly bodies soundlessly
Among a bright green world of weeds.
These thousand pebbles are a thousand eyes
Each sharper than the sun;
These waves are dancers;
Upon a thousand, pointed toes
They step the sea,
Lightly, as in a pantomime.

Dec 28ᵗʰ 1930

V

My golden bird the sun
Has spread his wings and flown away
Out of the swinging cage
You call the sky,
And, like his tired shadow
White with love,
My silver bird the moon
Flies up again
Onto her perch of stars.

December 30ᵗʰ 1930

VI

Live in my living;
When I am sad, be sad;
Take from our chaos
Few of your own wise smiles,
For I have merriment enough for both,
Too much for one to bear,
And, if we make it cruel laughter,
We shall have time,
A space of lies,
To show we can be kind.
Here is your breast,
And here is mine;
This is your foot,
And this is mine;
But live,
In all I offer for a little thing
So small you can but give it.

VII

Rain cuts the place we tread,
A sparkling fountain for us
With no fountain boy but me
To balance on my palms
The water from a street of clouds.
We sail a boat upon the path,
Paddle with leaves
Down an ecstatic line of light,
Watching, not too aware
To make our senses take too much,
The unrolled waves
So starred with gravel,
The living vessels of the garden
Drifting in easy time;
And, as we watch, the rainbow's foot

Stamps on the ground,
A legendary horse with hoof and feather,
Impatient to be off.
He goes across the sky,
But, when he's out of sight,
The mark his flying tail has left
Branches a million shades,
A gay parabola
Above a boat of leaves and weeds.
We try to steer;
The stream's fantastically hard,
Too stiff to churn with leaves,
A sedge of broken stalks and shells.
This is a drain of iron plants,
For when we touch a flower with our oar
We strike but do not stir it.
Our boat is made to rise
By waves which grow again
Their own melodious height,
Into the rainbow's shy embrace.
We shiver uncomplainingly,
And taste upon our lips, this minute,
The emerald caress,
And breath on breath of indigo.

Jan 2 1931

VIII

The morning, space for Leda
To stir the water with a buoyant foot,
And interlude for violins
To catch her sailing down the stream –
The phrases on the wood aren't hers;
A fishing bird has notes of ivory
Alive within his craning throat –
Sees the moon still up,
Bright, well-held head,

And, for a pivot,
The shadows from the glassy sea
To wet the sky with tears,
And daub the unrisen sun with longing.
The swan makes strings of water in her wake;
Between the moon and sun
There's time to pluck a tune upon the harp,
Moisten the mouth of sleep
To kiss awake
My hand with honey that had closed upon a flower.
Between the rising and the falling
Spring may be green –
Under her cloth of trees no sorrow,
Under her grassy dress no limbs –
And winter follow like an echo
The summer voice so warm from fruit
That clustered round her shoulders,
And hid her uncovered breast.
The morning, too, is time for love,
When Leda, on a toe of down,
Dances invisibly, a swan to see
Who holds her clasped inside his strong, white wings;
And darkness, hand in hand with light,
Is blind with tears too frail to taste.

Jan 20th. 1931

IX

The spire cranes; its statue
Is an aviary,
And from the nest
Of stone not straw
He does not let the nightingales
Blunt their tawny necks on rock,
Or pierce the sky with diving –
So wing in weed
And foot an inch in froth.

The bell's chimes cheat the sun,
And drop in time,
Induced to fall
Like discs upon the water,
Tune for the swimmer's hands
And silver music for his bubbling mouth.
But let him keep his faculties.
The spire's hook drops birds and notes,
Each featherless and stony hearted;
The upward birds are choice for you,
And notes that breast the vertical,
Or run the corridor on ladder,
Not tread the cloudy steps like prodigals.

27ᵗʰ Jan.

X

Cool may she find the day,
And the night full of singing;
No snow may fall
But she shall feel it so,
Cool for her sinking wrist,
Melodious for her ear.
A pleasant fall, the robin says,
White as your neck.
But if she grieves –
Though tears shan't blunt her joy –
Let sorrow come down with the snow,
'For you', the robin's voice.

XI

Yesterday, the cherry sun
Hung in its space until the steel string snapped,
The voice lost edge,
And the guitar was put away,
Dropping from the window
Into the paper sea,
A silver dog, a gypsy's hoop.
The handle's turned this time;
The sun again, you pretty fruit,
I almost touch it, press you, vein for vein,
But other tunes meet mine,
Turned by the handles,
Suave on their chiming stilts.
Your serenade upon machines,
The fifty discs that soar to you
In notes like stone-made circles
Growing larger, tick by tick,
Should make you glad;
Your face is pale,
And when I catch your rays
Upon the garden fork,
The beds aren't bathed with light,
And the crocus does not cry for shade.
The handle and the clockwork turn,
But the nightingale
Does not please the emperor;
I pluck again
The sweet, steel strings
To bring the sun to life,
Laugh at the echo made,
The steel bird put away,
Guitar in hand.

22ᵈ February 1931

XII

Time enough to rot;
Toss overhead
Your golden ball of blood;
Breathe against air,
Puffing the light's flame to and fro,
Not drawing in your suction's kiss.
Your mouth's fine dust
Will find such love against the grain.
And break through dark;
It's acrid in the streets;
A paper witch upon her sulphured broom
Flies from the gutter.
The still go hard,
The moving fructify;
The walker's apple's black as sin;
The waters of his mind draw in.
   Then swim your head,
   For you've a sea to lie.

*Feb 24**th*

                XIII

Conceive these images in air,
Wrap them in flame, they're mine;
Set against granite,
Let the two dull stones be grey,
Or, formed of sand,
Trickle away through thought,
In water or in metal,
Flowing and melting under lime.
Cut them in rock,
So, not to be defaced,
They harden and take shape again
As signs I've not brought down
To any lighter state
By love-tip or my hand's red heat.

*March 20**th*

XIV

You be my hermaphrodite in logic,
My avocado temptress out of magic –
For who can keep illusions up
Before such honest chemistry
As turns love like a ring
From tip to cavity –
And when, in tune with me,
You're lost to sense,
With what coincidence
I'll rip your kiss from me,
And force you to a different sex.
The change will do my conscience good,
Before it blunts my tongue
And hurts whatever knows the joy
Of such cerebral sodomy.
There's truth in every word, there's gaiety,
To germinate in each chaotic move
Beyond the region of the mouth,
There's truth for the voluptuary
Inside satiety, or out of hate.
How is the cynic cancerized.
He cannot laugh with me at me;
He laughs from him at me;
We laugh at him with words and blood
Or paint and wood,
Safe in our wise orgasm,
Mind after body to endeavour.

24th March.

XV

Until the light is less,
And pity's shoulder-high
And full of sugar –
But does the waist entice,
Sweet smile sweet
Longer than time to meet the lips? –
Each gap for love lies heavily.
And you disturb the paradox,
That asks for water when it's wet.
Love's to the brim;
More love shan't spoil the balance,
But rather thin the growing waves
Into their shade
Upon the careless lines.
No wrong in pity through the eyes,
Or even from the tongue
Wet with such speech
As turns the flaccid heart the wrong way up,
When your old look makes moisture,
Scalds, harms, and buries
Within an intake's age.
So pat my hand,
And many times
In temperament with me,
Kiss on the ulcer
Till it learns to ache.
We're side by side,
Inches from home and yards from heaven,
You with an ageing glance,
And I, in pain and utter friendliness,
With little words to make forget,
Knowledge, no knowledge.

March 28ᵗʰ

73

XVI

The neophyte, baptized in smiles,
Is laughing boy beneath his oath,
Breathing no poison from the oval mouth,
Or evil from the cankered heart.
Where love is there's a crust of joy
To hide what drags its belly from the egg,
And, on the ground, gyrates as easily
As though the sun were spinning up through it.
Boy sucks no sweetness from the willing mouth,
Nothing but poison from the breath,
And, in the grief of certainty,
Knows his love rots.
Outdo your prude's genetic faculty
That grew for good
Out of the bitter conscience and the nerves,
Not from the senses' dualizing tip
Of water, flame, or air.
Wetten your tongue and lip,
Moisten your care to carelessness,
For she who sprinkled on your brow
The shining symbols of her peace with you
Was old when you were young,
Old in illusions turned to acritudes,
And thoughts, be they so kind,
Touched, by a finger's nail, to dust.

April 6th '31

XVII

To be encompassed by the brilliant earth
Breathing on all sides pungently
Into her vegetation's lapping mouths
Must feel like such encroachment
As edges off your nerves to mine,
The hemming contact that's so trammelled

74

By love or look,
In death or out of death,
Glancing from the yellow nut,
Eyeing from the wax's tower,
Or, white as milk, out of the seeping dark,
The drooping as you close me in
A world of webs
I touch and break,
I touch and break.

10th *April 1931*

XVIII

Who is to mar
My lying long,
Or blow away its grains,
Across my lover's sandy bed,
Sick at the coming close,
Yet iron-white and loth to part,
Ascetic, letting the hand loll
Upon my sybarite's strong calf?
Who is to stop,
Or mend the growth
Of such unreason in a time of magic
Whose order calls the fairy out
To stem and step the light
Before the little day is dark as sense?
Who's the logician
Sucking my gay disgust
Through love to shape,
Wit wise and heady no man knows,
Of numbers beyond me,
Of numbers beyond you,
Who's to infer the tragedy?
When the sand's away
By wind to leave the metal,
Then shall the epicene take pride of place.

Now drown and let drown,
Yellow like honey seed
Falling below the water;
Now shall the graph be stained with salt;
And the crying gone,
The crying aloud that never can
In age or motion,
Or the time of the thin blood.

May 18th '31

XIX

The natural day and night
Are full enough to drown my melancholy
Of sound and sight,
Vigour and harmony in light to none,
One hour spend my time for me
In tuning impulses to calls;
Kinder;
So phrase;
Don't hurt the chic anatomy
Of ladies' needles worn to breaking point
Sewing a lie to a credulity,
With zest culled from their ladylike heat,
Hedgerow, laboratory, and even glasshouse,
But the sun cracks it
But the stones crack it
Out of my hand in stopping up my mouth,
My ears, my nose, my eyes,
And all my thin prerogative of taste.
But while day is there's night to it,
And night to it.
The black shadow comes down,
And the beautiful noise is quelled,
For my merry words,
So rare –
Who taught me trouble?

I, said the beetle, out of my thin black womb,
Out of my thin black lips,
Trouble enough for the world
Out of my filthy eyes
And my corrupting knowledge –
They are the words for weeping.
Crying aloud in pain,
Thick to the skull,
Oh gaiety!
Oh gaiety!
Penumbra derry,
Do the right thing to do the right;
Do, down a derry.

March 30ᵗʰ '31.

XX

Although through my bewildered way
Of crying off this unshaped evil,
Death to the magical when all is done,
Age come to you – you're bright and useless,
Soon to my care, my love,
But soon to die
In time, like all, through my unreason
In a gay moment's falsity –
There is no need of hope for hope,
You'll bring the place to me
Where all is well,
Noble among a crowd of lights.
Then shall your senses, out of joy,
Tingle on mine;
You're the perverse to lie across,
Out of the heart for me,
Sick, pale, and plain,
So that the process calls for laughs,
The silly binding
Snapped in a rain of pieces falling

On head and running foot,
For, if I could, I'd fly away,
For, if I could, I'd fly away
Before the last light is blown
Into the void again of this bewilderment and that insanity.

June 1st. '31

XXI

High on a hill,
Straddle and soak,
Out of the way of the eyes of men,
Out of the way,
Straddle her wrinkled knees
Until the day's broken –
Christ, let me write from the heart,
War on the heart –
Puff till the adder is,
Breathe till the snake is home,
Inch on the old thigh
Till the bird has burst his shell,
And the carnal stem that stood
Blowing with the blood's ebb,
Is fallen down
- To the ground.

June 1st '31

XXII

Refract the lady, drown the profiteer
Inside the angles of his sanguine cup.
If he is jew then rend his gaberdine,
If Christian cut him navel up.
Refract the lady, her visage bouncing
From cup to jew,

That vision dancing with tidy-knickered girl
For higher thrills than seeing limbs
And giving ices.
If he is jew, make him a christian swine,
If christian, ask him did christ mean
The christian jews to be unclean.

1931

XXIII

Into be home from home
And split the searching for the truth
Into a part for casuistry
And then a part for ghost or jew,
Of Islam's people
Paring the pennyweight of their accustomed love
For ghost or jew in the mythology,
A hundred times
And then a hundred times,
But Peter was a libertine.
The words are scattered down the canal
This time to rake hell
Until be nut-brown fiend – phonetic water
Washes to a wisp;
And I am all there is this second,
Genius for the chosen people
From the cross and hundred men,
And thief I am at His side.
I'll put away the clock,
Scorn, intone again, the pride there is
Of hanging up the blue grape,
Etching the mossy castle we lived in
When there was grass on Calvary,
And the children's pond
Fit for my sails or for my wings.
The truth is only half

The sour minute drawing mine,
Floating through pitch
A long way to the prophet,
(He is a man of letters
Who hates me for a proselyte
From no faith to fanatic),
Sidling to the wits' trapezium,
But when I call on the sweet substance
Mind what I do,
For Jesus was a social poem
For Jesus though his death's a logogram.

June 10th

XXIV

if the lady from the casino
will stop the flacillating roof
de paris and many women from my thinking
over the running bannisters
who can tell I may be strong enough
to push the floor away with a great gesture
but for the navels and the chandelebra
mending my coloned head in hands
And are you parallel in thinking good with me
Of us beneath the shepherd's crook
Driving the wolves away
And walking the metallic fields
An inch's time away with every step
Who has no hope
I know him for he lives in me
lady gap
they're there I see them
on railings and on pots of ferns
seeking a sex in me
beneath the nose.........
Iif its no beginning in our love
wise woman true for heat

it's no end to us
or even interlude between the abstract
and the side or shell
hindering my knuckles or my knife
our modern formula
of death to sense and dissolution
where there is love there's agony
Ttheres sex where our mad hands rest
. . . .
Of ever watching your light
Come to a point with mine
Your pity left me high and dry
For appetites aren't fed with
can they for ever
stop their navels with their finger tops
or
. . . . Bbranch off straight to nonsense narrow. . . . .
Hope ah I know it
one naked hand upon the bracket
out of the pages
would I blind in puberty the phrases
grow and here's a castle
Hope I knew him out of Rreason
Faith messiah for what death
though they do not speak like that in France;
But while I'm deft and aphrodisiac
To her who her the nought for my loud nerves
Not to the incubator or the brain
A mass of words above the window
Chiming for room
One brings you allonal
Which bells grotesque parade
Of leg on breast
And vomit on a shining cheek
Of masks *two* can't take off
But in its true light devil naturally
And let there be an end to
evil
I have an explanation

And what is more an egg
So with my mind's catastrophe
And white and yellow anna
Three has no message in his sin
And *four* a skull for tympani
Choked up with wit
The *rest* shall wait for not engendering
And I along the skin
Think of my passionate alloy
I cool who's chastity
now nothing yes loud purity
With
bawdy
Eyes and with the nerves' unrest
shatter the french
to let the Old Seduced crowd on
over the hurdle of the belly de
through mercy to paris
I'll in a moment but my version's sane
space is too small
hover along the saxophone
and tread the mandoline a navel's length
the women on the ground are dead
who her dont care for clothes
and I no longer itch at every trouble

16ᵗʰ June. '31

XXV

Through sober to the truth when
All hold out their aqueous hands,
Touching me low
By any frond of smiles,
And that's transition worth my toil.
I have a friend in death,
Daywise, the grave's inertia
Mending my head that needs its hour's pain

Under the arc-lamp,
Or between my skull and me.
Through truth again, and there's sobriety
Touching me low
By any smile shaped
From the solid hand, good death,
To regularity,
Making the paradox
This glass's spring
Veracity (I know your frond by smell).
The moment is so small
The beam that wakes the highing urge
A way off from its so true state
Can't hope to have
The molten sand's deep autumn
Blown by this wind to death.
I have a friend who sends
Irregular reprisal
To laughing, in a shape,
And love, all beams,
Upon a thistle,
Who is my friend in truth.
Sober, he heaps his shadows on my aching mind,
But, with the water on your hands,
He plays his sun a time too loud,
Deafens, and with his blood
Drowns all the actions have I lied.

July 3rd '31

XXVI

It is the wrong, the hurt, the mineral,
That makes its stroke
Through wisdom, for my age,
And sin, for my two-headed joy –
The particles aren't more than dust,
And whose affections aren't corrupt? –

83

Listen and lie;
The head's vacuity can breed no truth
Out of its sensible tedium,
But if chastity's a hybrid freak
From the shy evil
And the reeking courage known to all
Who spend their love, my paradox,
Within the places of the mind,
Sink head and heart
In feelings that shan't last a day,
For I shall turn the strongest stomach up
With filth I gather
From the thousand minds, all lust and wind,
Like a beachcomber in the time of light.
You are untouched, unhurt,
Corroded by an acid heart
That eats and lets eat
Till the loin is dumb
That spoke the woman's passion musically.
She is the evil in the good,
Out of reason to the shuddering care,
Breath, limb, and blood
Over what time I'll set upon
A bridge of being,
And you're the logical who knows the hurt,
The wrong, the wound, the mineral,
And you're the chemically chaste.

July 28ᵗʰ '31

XXVII

Even the voice will not last
Master can but vanish
Like a shaft no deader self it has
Refracting till the colour snaps
Time place and like a bell the chiming strength.
Even the patient eye and gesture
Meaning in the lightest touch

Upon the heart or flesh
And sense usurping use in this pasture
Of innocence that's built on ignorance
Will not see this instant's sun and moon out
Can't but vanish too
And leave such chaos
As will confuse the hush-voice left
As will confuse.
I look Sir at my adumbratic navel
Though what I see won't help progress
But rather pen me in a pleasant insularity
Unbalancing devoid of humour
And the wise thoughts wait until the sea is calmer;
Then can they scud as saillessly
Reach breathe and multiply
Within the chaos that my dying voice has helped
Has struck its note unknowing
And will again before it joins its gesture.
A footprint makes me homesick
For Glaucus or a scabrous hearth
For Pan and pot a novel death
Out of the names the cankered greeks.

Aug 2ᵈ '31

XXVIII

True love's inflated; from a truthful shape
Hope blew it to a cylinder
Of faithfulness where there is none
However true we are in falsities,
Of ease where there can never be
But pain,
Made big the busy lines,
The easy contours daft with symmetry.
But lest the metal prove too strong
And break resistance down –
A minute only,
Weak not too weak –

I'll draw invective for a truthful sake
From what has gone of wisdom in a touch.
But thank pollution if the cylinder,
O Love, becomes its shape again,
For what I do lies in your vainest heart
Which thrives on hope of more than I can offer,
Or anyone, or anyone
While there is time for time to age,
Make all sweet sour,
And there's time to die.

Aug: 8th '31

XXIX

Since, on a quiet night, I heard them talk
Who have no voices but the winds'
Of all the mystery there is in life
And all the mastery there is in death,
I have not lain an hour asleep
But troubled by their curious speech
Stealing so softly into the ears.
One says: There was a woman with no friend,
And, standing over the sea, she'd cry
Her loneliness across the empty waves
Time after time.
And every voice:
Oblivion is as loverless;
Oblivion is as loverless.
And then again: There was a child
Upon the earth who knew no joy,
For there was no light in his eyes,
And there was no light in his soul.
Oblivion is as blind,
Oblivion is as blind,
I hear them say out of the darkness
Who have no talk but that of death.

Aug: 12th '31

XXX

They are the only dead who did not love,
Lipless and tongueless in the sour earth
Staring at others, poor unlovers.
They are the only living who did love,
So are we full with strength,
Ready to rise, easy to sleep.
Who has completeness that can cut
A comic hour to an end through want of woman
And the warmth she gives,
And yet be human,
Feel the same soft blood flow thoroughly,
Have food and drink, unloving?
None, and his deadly welcome
At the hour's end
Shall prove unworthy for his doing,
Which was good at word,
But came from out the mouth unknowing
Of such great goodness as is ours.
There is no dead but is not loved
Awhile, a little,
Out of the fulness of another's heart
Having so much to spare.
That, then, is fortunate,
But, by your habit unreturned,
And by your habit unreturnable.
So is there missed a certain godliness
That's not without its woe,
And not without divinity,
For it can quicken or it can kill.

Look, there's the dead who did not love,
And there's the living who did love,
Around our little selves
Touching our separate love with badinage.

Aug 16th

87

XXXI

Have hold on my heart utterly,
Or let it go; pierce through and through
Or leave unpierced,
For I am faithless as the rest,
And would, if you not love
Strong this day unto its finish
When comes its age and loss, relinquish
All, and take what thing I offer
As blithely to another lover,
Confessing, though it woundeth much,
Our love as such that passes at a glance,
A moving, or an itch.
Not till the ripest fruit is fallen
Of what our meeting was,
And joy has given way to woe,
Not till there'll be a manner of regret
Springing out of the lithe morning
With every time of new caressing,
Oh, do not fear that I shall lessen
All that is old;
I warned you, lover, of a woeful host,
Of weariness at best and last;
Before death you should count the cost.

XXXII

The caterpillar is with child;
The leopard stirs his loin,
And there is temper in his cry,
And there is cunning in his stride,
A hard, sleek cataract of fear
Running through his yellow eyes,
Awareness of the insect's love,

A fibrous contact hard to touch
With paw, or side, or tongue.

Unless the sparrow's mating with the twig,
Their hands inlaced,
Here is your time that asks for reason;
The poor reply is lost in smiles,
The armadillo shaking his leather sides,
And Pierrot with a stolen Toby
Showing his teeth to Punch.
La la! Parisian lady,
You've a way with men,
And I've a way with words there's no denying,
But now I snap my fingers.
Do, do, a pet for bed;
Sleep with his fur upon your skin;
His tongue's for kissing.
When you were young...
   Too many songs,
   Too little tears,
Inflection in the rising voice
Means now it's over, and the sun's gone down.
Play on my mouth,
Or blow along a bird's feather.

January 1931

XXXIII

Foot, head, or traces
Are on sandy soil their spirit level;
Their level is the length
Of foot or head we'll be the time
In tracing
For a purpose (head to foot is head and foot,
        No wit, is one),
That'll make, it's brittle, diaphragm
For use of sense (no hurt no sense).

Foot head compressed,
It's easy tracing what each gives the other
By toe or foot to common good
           (Good for can run
           And know why run),
Though, after's done, I
See the reason for undoubling doubling not,
Unless for poetry, which, if it asks me
For a spirit, can
Run and know why
And know why know, no wit,
Can ever further,
Though no ask brings it
For a lazy sake that won't create
But plumb such depths as you,
Original, derive.

18ᵗʰ August '31

XXXV

Or be my paramour or die,
Lie or be lost to love,
Give up your gravity
Holding a too-heavy heart,
And take a gaiety without regret.
For let love go by a time
It goes for ever,
Each lightest kiss the last
From one or any lover,
Each single motion of the hand,
The head, the breast, is unrepeated,
And the body, not to last, has not kith nor ghost.

XXXVI

The womb and the woman's grave
Lie near, the thumb and thread
Are gone – no labour'll thrive
Which asketh not from God
Some strength no labour has.
Womb was for life she gave,
And woman was;
Grave was for death she hath.
She takes and she returns
From God and then to God,
Gives what her body had
And takes a little death from Him
Not one man can.

XXXVII

Let Sheba bear a love for Solomon
Out of her woman's heart and her content
That bridges time and like the morning sun
Lays its bright rod on all contempt,
For she was young in years and rich in fare,
Woman as you are woman but love dies –
The song of Solomon upon the ways of men,
Love dies, dies as the rose or fruit,
Leaf, hand, or animal,
Is and is not,
The words that bridge content and time,
Is and is not.

XXXVIII

There was one world and there is another,
For in our life we're dead as wood,
No bones or blood,
Out of a wooden mother,
And in our death learning such truth
As thought and told
That wood shall rot, but wood shan't rot.
The heavy night we breathe's unlit
When the heart stops,
Unstarred when the veins are chill,
And, night or night, the same remorse
Heavy on head and heart,
Oblivion or oblivion, the same heartbreak
Under and over the earth.

XXXIX

For us there cannot be welcome
For sleep at the day's end or the night's end
For many a time of tiredness,
For welcoming sleep we welcome death,
And death's an end to sleep,
And sleep to death, an end to love,
Ending and sleeping,
Love sleeps and ends for it cannot last.
And if we love we sleep,
Love, sleep, and end, for
Love is sleep, and ends and sleeps;
All can be compassed thus therein,
Love, sleep, and death the only plan.

Sept 11th

XL

An end to substance in decay's a sequence
Showing here and there a sign of wear,
Used as it is by man and beast,
Turned by the artist to an alchemy,
So we have tired of dying,
Tired like Lot of the flesh
But turning it not to salt but to romance,
And with one gesture
Drowning the hare-lipped gods
For one unstained to rise up from the depths.
Mother who bore me loved unchemically,
Mixing her acids with a man's
For other than a physic urge,
And I borne from her pain
Have, too, coarsened another's blood.
So are we tired of reality;
My rubber hands upon your flesh
Owe nothing to it,
Wise, spiritual hands; our reek is scent;
Our sweat is wine,
And all our dropping blood's symbolic.
Let's prick the young man he can't bleed,
But a stream of thin water will flow from him,
Let's kill the young man he don't care
For without any blood he don't wish to live,
And who took his blood and who took his blood
And you took his blood, and I took his blood,
Wanting to die for we got no blood,
No guts or no bones to catch on the stones.
Take an emetic, some strong emotion,
Suck it down deep with no reaction,
Do not be steady for that was the ruin of me.
I think I am steady for a time
Not savage any more but steady
I who am steady was once savage
I was savage but now I am steady.

Sept 11th

XLI

Why is the blood red and the grass green
Shan't be answered till the voice is still
That drieth the veins with its moan
Of man and his meaning, for the voice is cruel
That drieth the veins from the vines
And the blood from the high hills.
It shall be Job's voice or Israel's voice,
Or the voice from the wilderness,
That crieth for reason till the night is won
Or the still night begun,
And man has no meaning, for the blood says,
And who taught it red, and the grass which is green.
He has no meaning but the blood's.
Shall it be wise then to make a mystery of nothing ·
Until the mysterious blood is questioned?
He has no meaning but the blood's;
He has no knowing, be he wiser than his veins,
Of love and the passing of time,
A breath, step and gesture; he lifteth his hand
But he is not seen.

Sept: 12th

XLII

Have cheated constancy
Of mood and love,
Have worn stuff thin
That made air fit to breathe
And the dark brain cool
When lover lay for man to touch
Untouched by any other,
Have cheated mood, have not been chaste.
Shall we then suffer
For the cauldron of the brain's not cool
Through lover leaving man for other kisses

Soft as they were soft upon the cavernous lips?
Have cheated constancy,
Am knave stealing all to give nothing,
Lover untouched by any but all,
And the dark brain's cool again
Under a second constancy
Of lover, lover, and the soft-lipped lover.

21ˢᵗ September '31

XLIII

There's plenty in the world that doth not die,
And much that lives to perish,
That rises and then falls, buds but to wither;
The season's sun, though he should know his setting
Up to the second of the dark coming,
Death sights and sees with no misgiving
A rib of cancer on the fluid sky.
But we, shut in the houses of the brain,
Brood on each hothouse plant
Spewing its sapless leaves around,
And watch the hand of time unceasingly
Ticking the world away,
Shut in the madhouse call for cool air to breathe.
There's plenty that doth die;
Time can not heal nor resurrect;
And yet, mad with young blood or stained with age,
We still are loth to part with what remains,
Feeling the wind about our heads that does not cool,
And on our lips the dry mouth of the rain.
Plenty that dieth like to man and his;
Death take us all and close the tired lids.

September 24ᵗʰ '31

XLIV

This time took has much
In breath and width with that
Old other known as pressure,
For it's love one word or not,
Though call it god and hurt me,
Heat and offend the widow,
Each to his separate lesson
To mould, alone, masonic reason.
And baby-do is baby-come,
Out of the infant's mouth
Learn what is infant truth,
See what the boy writes on the wall,
The facts of being in a doggerel.
This time took
Holds the same lie as any girl's,
Love's a descension of the drawers
An earlier time and now;
Pressure may change,
The widow's word confess to age,
And mine be burnt with vinegar,
Shall not disturb or alter,
Breath with the girl's or regular.

Sept: 30th '31

XLV

Which of you put out his rising,
And turned his flame into a blind wick,
Of you pale-minded virgins which shook down your tress
Onto his lifted face, who is so pitiless,
Can wipe away the thought of passion like a crumb,
Hates him for loving, hates him,
Who, narrow-necked, broke all his heart,
Left it among the cigarette-ends and the glasses?
Would for a moment she conceal all else,

96

And open out to him her grassy arms
With, 'Undisturbed, loin undisturbed
On lap for pillow, of the moving breast,
Peace on thy resting head'.
O women, lead him by the hand;
O women, lead me by the hand;
Take this my hand;
Take this his hand.

October 15th.

XLVI

Written for a Personal Epitaph

Feeding the worm
Who do I blame
Because laid down
At last by time,
Here under the earth with girl and thief,
Who do I blame?
Mother I blame
Whose loving crime
Moulded my form
Within her womb,
Who gave me life and then the grave,
Mother I blame.
Here is her labour's end,
Dead limb and mind,
All love and sweat
Gone now to rot.
I am man's reply to every question,
His aim and destination.

17th Oct '31

XLVII

When you have ground such beauty down to dust
As flies before the breath
And, at the touch, trembles with lover's fever,
Or sundered it to look the closer,
Magnified and made immense
At one side's loss,
Turn inside out, and see at glance
Wisdom is folly, love is not,
Sense can but maim it, wisdom mar it,
Folly purify and make it true.
For folly was
When wisdom lay not in the soul
But in the body of the trees and stones,
Was when sense found a way to them
Growing on hills or shining under water.
Come wise in foolishness,
Go silly and be Christ's good brother,
He whose lovers were both wise and sensible
When folly stirred, warm in the foolish heart.

Oct: 10th '31

XLVIII

Sever from what I trust
The things, this time, I love,
Death and the shy entanglement of sense
Crying for age to bless its sad sobriety;
It's blind and out of tune,
Moving symmetrically in chaos
Day through till we're all older,
Wise to the seasons' touch on us
Of hope, and time, and sun.
Death out of sense,

Then what I love I trust,
And, careless child again,
Am, from your look and smile,
Same head-in-air.

July '31

XLIX

Never to reach the oblivious dark
And not to know
Any man's troubles nor your own –
Negatives impress negation,
Empty of light and find the darkness lit –
Never is nightmare,
Never flows out from the wound of sleep
Staining the broken brain
With knowledge that no use and nothing worth
Still's vain to argue after death;
No use to run your head against the wall
To find a sweet blankness in the blood and shell,
This pus runs deep.
There's poison in your red wine, drinker,
Which spreads down to the dregs
Leaving a corrupted vein of colour,
Sawdust beneath the skirts;
On every hand the evil's positive
For dead or live,
Froth or a moment's movement
All hold the sum, nothing to nothing,
Even the words are nothing
While the sun's turned to salt,
Can be but vanity, such an old cry,
Nothing never, nothing older
Though we're consumed by loves and doubts.
I love and doubt, it's vain, it's vain,

99

Loving and doubting like one who is to die
Planning what's good, though it's but winter,
When spring is come,
The jonquil and the trumpet.

Oct 26th

L

Introductory Poem

So that his philosophy be proven
Let the philosopher go to the oven,
And the wise man from the fools
Escape under the motor-wheels.
Thus I defy all poetry
By staying in this aviary.

October

LI

Take up this seed, it is most beautiful,
Within its husk opening in fire and air
Into a flower's stem and a flower's mouth,
To lean upon the wall of summer
And touch the lips of the dark wind.
Lift up this seed; life from its circle
Spins towards light,
Full-voiced from many seasons' sounds
And, in a fruit's fall or a bird's fall,
Is one with all plants in the earth's well,
Such is its miracle.
Touch these broad leaves, all fiery-veined,
Touch these green leaves and this fair stalk;
Fair as they are the seed is fairer,
Budding to light out of its own darkness;
What once was hot beneath the earth's as cool as rain,

100

As sweet as rain, as falling soft as snow;
What lay unknowing in the soil
Of any weariness at all
Now droops and sleeps at the day's end,
And at its hour's end lets death be friend and comforter.
What once was beautiful is dead,
Was sweet is sour.

LII

There in her tears were laughter and tears again,
O so unstable, never to love for long
While the body's full of the heart's pain
And the heart breaks down
A mechanism oiled with lily's sap
And weighed with age,
O so unstable, no time is actual.

I know this minute counts in the blood
Rising to the nerves' rim to fall again
But in the heart no easy pyramid,
O so unstable, in the blood and brain
But in the heart no more than water
Than tears which flow with laughter,
O so unstable, which will run with tears.

November 3rd '31

LIII

How can the knotted root
Be trapped in a snare of syllables,
The tendril or, what's stranger, the high flower
Caught, like a ferret though a thought it is,
Inside a web of words,
Taken for good, each moving feature?
Get your gardener in some notes,

101

But not his thoughts
Creaking on barrow-wheels along the gravel,
They won't be stopped or snared;
Spoon them about with honey,
His or mine, they're easier stuck than barred in;
Easier to have a ferret than a bird in,
So lay on sweet words,
Lay on neat words,
The only way the world knows;
I have you in my dung as inescapably
As you in your hive, and quite as capably.

5ᵗʰ & 6ᵗʰ Nov '31

LIV

Children of darkness got no wings,
This we know we got no wings,
Stay, dramatic figures, tethered down
By weight of cloth and fact,
Crystal or funeral, got no hope
For us that knows misventure
Only as wrong; but shan't the genius fail,
Gliding, rope-dancing, is his fancy,
Better nor us can't gainsay walking,
Who'll break our necks upon the pavement
Easier than he upon the ice.
For we are ordinary men,
Sleep, wake, and sleep, eat, love, and laugh,
With wide, dry mouths and eyes,
Poor, petty vermin,
Stink of cigarettes and armpits,
Cut our figures, and retreat at night
Into a double or a single bed,
The same thoughts in our head.
We are ordinary men,
Bred in the dark behind the skirting-board,

Crying with hungry voices in our nest.

Children of darkness got no wings,
This we know, we got no wings,
Stay, in a circle chalked upon the floor,
Waiting all vainly this we know.

October.

LV

It's not in misery but in oblivion,
Not vertically in a mood of joy
Screaming the spring
Over the ancient winter,
He'll lie down, and our breath
Will chill the roundness of his cheeks,
And make his wide mouth home.
For we must whisper down the funnel
The love we had and glory in his blood
Coursing along the channels
Until the spout dried up
That flowed out of the soil
All seasons with the same meticulous power,
But the veins must fail.
He's not awake to the grave
Though we cry down the funnel,
Splitting a thought into such hideous moments
As drown, over and over, this fever.
He's dead, home, has no lover,
But our speaking does not thrive
In the bosom, or the empty channels.
Our evil, when we breathe it,
Of dissolution and the empty fall,
Won't harm the tent around him,
Uneaten and not to be pierced
By us in sin or us in gaiety.

103

And who shall tell the amorist
Oblivion is so loverless?

March. '31

LVI

What lunatic's whored after shadow,
Followed the full-voiced stream
To stoop and taste it vinegar,
Can find the body anything but shade,
That, too, wet with his tears,
And anything but acid the clear water?
He shall be fed with dreams till there's no other food
But sickens or sits wearily,
Shall look for woman,
And shall lie with cloud.
Then has the written word
To give the love he haggard lacked from her,
The lifted note and the carven stone
Be his mate, and his kiss, and his company.

Mad, mad, praising the sweep from neck to breasts,
This woman's celluloid; drip your contagious thoughts
Into the basin;
Mad, mad with other's lunacy
That pares the substance off the rind,
Hot with their written heat,
And when the page is turned, oh stone, cold stone!
None know why the heart is vexed,
And the lax brain,
When loving means nothing, housed in the bosom
Man feels no safety in his heart,
And goes away, and goes away.
Lunatic, was she not mate, and kiss, and company?
She was all that to me.

November '31

LVII

Here is a fact for my teeth
That I've snapped off the bone,
Robs death of its comforter,
That bites good and deep,
There's much sense in sleep.
I own negation, we are the lie-a-bed,
Lie-a-lap, wind-in-our-heads,
Knowing all's nothing,
Worth nothing, ends nothing,
We own negation.
Head in the oven, no nearer heaven,
Full-veined, we may be empty,
The good we get
In slowly for an empty end
Senselessly lifting food to mouth, and food to mouth,
To keep the senseless being going.

LVIII

Any matter move it to conclusion
Begs for a refuge with the bone
So any talk carefree as words can
Down in the sweet-smelling earth
Takes start and end into the warmth
All argument speaker not a nickel's worth

And handymaid shall split the apple
For Eve and her soft-bellied both
And ladling or half-leaved
Both fit for bull and man
Bull not complaining and man shall not envy
Eve's and her evil not for a moment's thought.

Any matter start it with levity
Brevity poetry

Brimmed with sure fire spit it up
Out and the air's as fresh as cider-cheek
Breast fit for sipping and chin to chuck.

January '32

LVIV

Too long, skeleton, death's risen
Out of the soil and seed into the drive,
Chalk cooled by leaves in the hot season,
Too long, skeleton, death's all alive
From nape to toe, a sanatorium piece
Clean as a whistle, rid of fleas.

Take now content, no longer posturing
As raped and reaped, the final emblem.
Thy place is filled, bones bid for auction,
The prism of the eye now void by suction,
New man best whose breast hangs low,
Rather than charnel-house as symbol
Of the moment and the dead hour.

Jan 20 '32

LVV

No man knows loveliness at all,
Though he be beauty blessed,
Who has not known the loveliness of May,
The blossoms and the throated trees
Lifting their branches lit with singing birds
Into the laden air;
Neither can woman, though she be peacock-fair,

And, like the peacock, proudly dressed,
Know all of love who has not known this lovers' season.

What can I make out of it all,
Flowers, trees, birds, and so much singing?
No man, I said, knows loveliness at all,
Nor woman love.
But this is true, and the high words
Flutter to the ground beside this truth.

April '32

LVVI

Do thou heed me, cinnamon smelling,
Crying my blind love across the brain,
With every tingling nerve
Bidding thee bend who will not kiss and mate.
Vein calls to vein but the heart says vanity,
Colder she is than the water's face;
Cinnamon-smelling,
Print my kiss on thy left breast and thy right.

(Fragment. April '32.)

LVVII

They said, tired of trafficking,
The sea moves and man moves blind,
While the sea moved calm
And man, obsessed,
Moved like a mole within his fleshy prison,
Taking how gladly the lips' poison,
And, as they told, obsessed
With drink and work, the tame machines,
Money, graft, lust and incest.
All this to drive him mad, they said,

Too blind, mad, too, themselves,
Men in disease and women mad in hospitals.
The world is growing up,
And what fits father'll fit the world,
Will hurt they said, but will be worn,
Is growing up to be a man,
Though man, their logic, is both daft and drunk,
And cannot close his eaten lids.

May 5 1932.

LVVIII

Be silent let who will
Speak ill of age
Who does not advocate
The oven or the old adage
Drink and be merry
Tom Dick and Harry
For tomorrow if not dead
One's old or mad.

May '32

LVVIV

Being but men, we walked into the trees
Afraid, letting our syllables be soft
For fear of waking the rooks,
For fear of coming
Noiselessly into a world of wings and cries.

If we were children we might climb,
Catch the rooks sleeping, and break no twig,
And, after the soft ascent,

Thrust out our heads above the branches
To wonder at the unfailing stars.

Out of confusion, as the way is,
And the wonder that man knows,
Out of the chaos would come bliss.

That, then, is loveliness, we said,
Children in wonder watching the stars,
Is the aim and the end.

Being but men we walked into the trees.

May 7th '32

LVVV

The hunchback in the park,
A solitary mister
Propped between trees and water,
Going daft for fifty seven years,
Is going dafter,
A cripple children call at,
Half-laughing, by no other name than mister,
They shout hey mister
Running when he has heard them clearly
Past lake and rockery
On out of sight.

There is a thing he makes when quiet comes
To the young nurses with the children
And the three veteran swans,
Makes a thing inside the hanging head,
Creates a figure without fault

109

And sees it on the gravel paths
Or walking on the water.

The figure's frozen all the winter
Until the summer melts it down
To make a figure without fault.
It is a poem and it is a woman figure.

Mister, the children call, hey mister,
And the hunchback in the park
Sees the molten figure on the water,
Misty, now mistier,
And hears its woman's voice;
Mister, it calls, hey mister,
And the hunchback smiles.

May 9th '32

LVVVI

Out of the sighs a little comes,
But not of grief for I have vanquished that
Before the agony. The spirit grows,
Forgets, and cries.
A little comes, is tasted and found good;
All could not disappoint;
There must, be praised, some certainty,
If not of loving well, then not,
And that is true after perpetual defeat.

After such fighting as the weakest know
There's more than dying;
He'll lose the pain or stuff the wound,
But ache too long through no regret
Of leaving woman waiting, saving, lying,
For her warrior stained with split words
That spill such acrid blood.

June 7

Here is a beauty on a bough I can't translate
Through words or love,
So high it is, a bird unto his mate
Singing to prove
That in each note she lives for him again
A fledgling in the fall of winter rain.
Him would I be if to your mind
I could but sing for proof
That, though to you my crying soul's assigned,
I hold aloof,
Seeing a thousand times your bright smile glance
Across to me, without your love, and all by chance.

At last, in hail and rain,
The family failings lose the gain
Made by these ten years' reading:
Enterprise, machine, and devildom
All windward of the cleft skies.

Rain blew the man down
Who could not stand such strain,
For work to live is work to die,
And labour's lost in venom.

The collier lad has found his master;
He is a rake on holiday,
But master goes prancing from a family malady
To words or melody,
Smiling with cigarette and stick,
Going no place, no place at all.

May.

Upon your held-out hand
Count the endless days until they end,
Feel, as the pulse grows tired,
The angels' wings beating about your head
Unsounding, they beat so soft.
Why count so sadly?
Learn to be merry with the merriest,
Or (change the key!) give vent to utterances
As meaningless as the bells (oh change the life!),
The sideboard fruit, the ferns, the picture houses
And the pack of cards.

When I was seven I counted four and forty trees
That stood before my window,
Which may or not be relevant
And symbolize the maddening factors
That madden both watchers and actors.
I've said my piece: count or go mad.
The new asylum on the hill
Leers down the valley like a fool
Waiting and watching for your fingers to fail
To keep count of the stiles
The thousand sheep
Leap over to my criss-cross rhythms.
I've said my piece.

June 25 '32

Nearly summer, and the devil
Still comes visiting his poor relations,
If not in person sends his unending evil
By messengers, the flight of birds
Spelling across the sky his devil's news,
The seasons' cries, full of his intimations.
He has the whole field now, the gods departed
Who cannot count the seeds he sows,
The law allows,
His wild carouses, and his lips

Pursed at the ready ear
To whisper, when he wants, the senses' war
Or lay the senses' rumour.
The welcome devil comes as guest,
Steals what is best – the body's splendour –
Rapes, leaves for lost (the amorist!),
Counts on his fist
All he has reaped in wonder.

The welcome devil comes invited,
Suspicious but that soon passes.
They cry to be taken, and the devil breaks
All that is not already broken,
Leaves it among the cigarette ends and the glasses.

April '32

Pome

How the birds had become talkative,
No longer criss-cross on the sky
Or flying – lo there razor foot –
Near to water – lo there foam foe
Bruising the long waves with thy wing –,
On branches over his metal shoulder
Crouching and talking,
But for his cold intelligence
Breaking the sky with song.
To him they trilled, running their golden ladders up and down;
He heard no syllables,
And so missed what divinity
Their messages could hold for man unmaidened
And with helmet multiplying sun on sun
Till all the metal was parhelion.

June '32

Were that enough, enough to ease the pain,
Feeling regret when this is wasted
That made me happy in the sun
And, sleeping, made me dream
How much was happy while it lasted,
Were vaguenesses enough, and the sweet lies plenty,
Then hollow words could bear all suffering,
And cure me of ills.
Were this enough – bone, blood, and sinew,
The twisted brain, the fair formed loin,
Groping for matter under the dog's plate –
Man should be cured of distemper.
For all there is to give I offer:
Crumbs, barn, and halter.

July 1

Typescript Poems

For the seven months from July 1932 to January 1933 there is no extant notebook. Among the poems Thomas typed up and took with him to London in August 1933 (now in the British Library), there are eight that very likely came from a missing notebook for that period. They exhibit a fairly consistent attitude to life, a new social awareness, an expansion into political consciousness. It was in 1932 that Thomas met A. E. (Bert) Trick, the left-wing grocer, a member of Swansea Labour Party, who influenced the young poet greatly. He is the Mr Humphries of "Where Tawe Flows" in *Portrait of the Artist as a Young Dog* who spoke with Marxist scorn about the plight of the average man of the 1930s: 'Capitalist society has made him a mere bumble of repressions and useless habits under that symbol of middle-class divinity, the bowler' (p. 143). This earnest voice speaking of 'the ceaseless toil for bread and butter, the ogres of unemployment, the pettifogging gods of gentility, the hollow lies of the marriage bed' is listing a good number of the themes found in the eight poems we presume to be from a missing notebook of 1932.

(i)

Walking in gardens by the sides
Of marble bathers toeing the garden ponds,
Skirting the ordered beds of paint-box flowers,
We spoke of drink and girls, for hours
Touched on the outskirts of the mind,
Then stirred a little chaos in the sun.
A new divinity, a god of wheels
Destroying souls and laying waste,
Trampling to dust the bits and pieces
Of faulty men and their diseases,
Rose in our outworn brains. We spoke our lines,
Made, for the bathers to admire,
Dramatic gestures in the air.
Ruin and revolution
Whirled in our words, then faded.
We might have tried light matches in the wind.
Over and round the ordered garden hummed,
There was no need of a new divinity,
No tidy flower moved, no bather gracefully
Lifted her marble foot, or lowered her hand
To brush upon the waters of the pond.

(ii)

Now the thirst parches lip and tongue,
The dry fever burns until no heart is left,
Now is decay in bone and sinew,
When heaven – open wide the gates – has taken flight,
Searing the sky for thunderbolts to fall
On a man and mountain,
Is treason's time and the time of envy.

The acid pours away, the acid drips
Into the places and the crevices

117

Most fit for lovers to make harmony,
To catch the lovers' palsy,
And on the sweethearts' bed to lie and grin,
To smirk at love's undress,
Make mock of woman's meat,
And drown all sorrows in the gross catastrophe.

(iii)

Lift up your face, light
Breaking, stare at the sky
Consoling for night by day
That chases the ghosts of the trees
And the ghosts of the brain,
Making fresh what was stale
In the unsleeping mummery
Of men and creatures horribly
Staring at stone walls.
Lift up your head, let
Comfort come through the devils' clouds,
The nightmare's mist
Suspended from the devils' precipice,
Let comfort come slowly, lift
Up your hand to stroke the light,
Its honeyed cheek, soft-talking mouth,
Lift up the blinds over the blind eyes.

Out of unsleeping cogitations,
When the skeleton of war
Is with the corpse of peace,
(Notes not in sympathy, discord, unease),
The only visitor,
Must come content.
Therefore lift up, see, stroke the light.
Content shall come after a twisted night
If only with sunlight.

(iv)

Let it be known that little live but lies,
Love-lies, and god-lies, and lies-to-please,
Let children know, and old men at their gates,
That this is lies that moans departure,
And that is lies that, after the old men die,
Declare their souls, let children know, live after.

(v)

The midnight road, though young man tread unknowing,
Harbouring some thought of heaven, or haven hoping,
Yields peace and plenty at the end. Or is it peace,
This busy jarring on the nerves yet no outbreak?
And this is plenty, then, cloves and sweet oils, the bees' honey,
Enough kind food, enough kind speaking,
A film of people moving,
Their hands outstretched, to give and give?
And now behind the screen are vixen voices,
The midnight figures of a sulphurous brood
Stepping in nightmare on a nightmare's edges.
Above them poise the swollen clouds
That wait for breaking and that never break,
The living sky, the faces of the stars.

(vi)

With windmills turning wrong directions,
And signposts pointing up and down
Towards destruction and redemption,
No doubt the wind on which the rooks
Tumble, not flying, is false,
Plays scurvy tricks with values and intentions,
Guides and blows wickedly, for larks

119

Find hard to dart against a cloud,
To London's turned, and thirsty loads
Of men with flannel shirts
And girls with flowered hats
Intent on visiting the famous spots,
Ride in their charabancs on roads
That lead away to dirty towns
Dirtier with garages and cheap tea signs.

Faith in divinity would solve most things,
For then the wrong wind certainly
Would be the devil's wind, and the high trinity
Be guiltless of the windy wrongs.

But ways have changed, and most ways lead
To different places than were said
By those who planned the obvious routes
And now, mistaking the direction,
On miles of horizontal milestones,
Perplexed beyond perplexion,
Catch their poor guts.

The wind has changed, blown inside out
The coverings of dark and light,
Made meaning meaningless. The wrong wind stirs,
Puffed, old with venom, from a crusted mouth.
The changed wind blows, and there's a choice of signs.

To Heaven's turned, and pious loads
Of neophytes take altered roads.

(vii)

The gossipers have lowered their voices,
Willing words to make the rumours certain,
Suspicious hands tug at the neighbouring vices,
Unthinking actions given causes
Stir their old bones behind cupboard and curtain.

Putting two and two together,
Informed by rumour and the register,
The virgins smelt out, three streets up,
A girl whose single bed held two
To make ends meet,
Found managers and widows wanting
In morals and full marriage bunting,
And other virgins in official fathers.

For all the inconvenience they make,
The trouble, devildom, and heartbreak,
The withered women win them bedfellows.
Nightly upon their wrinkled breasts
Press the old lies and old ghosts.

(viii)

Especially when the November wind
With frosty fingers punishes my hair,
Or, beaten on by the straight beams of the sun,
I walk abroad, feeling my youth like fire
Burning weak blood and body up,
Does the brain reel, drunk on the raw
Spirits of words, and the heart sicken
Of arid syllables grouped and regrouped with care,

Of the chosen task that lies upon
My belly like a cold stone.

By the sea's side hearing the cries of gulls,
In winter fields hearing a sheep cough
That wakes out of tubercular oblivion
Into a wet world, my heart rebels
Against the chain of words,
Now hard as iron and now soft as clouds,
While weighted trees lift asking arms far off.

Shut in a tower of words, I mark
Men in the distance walk like trees
And talking as the four winds talk,
Children in parks and children's homes
Speaking on fingers and thumbs,
And think, as drummed on by the sun,
How good it is to feel November air
And be no words' prisoner.

To view the changing world behind
A pot of ferns, lifting the sunblind
See gilded people walking on hindlegs
Along the pavement where a blind man begs
Hopefully, helplessly, feeling the sun's wings,
To trim a window garden with a shears,
To read front pages, fall asleep,
Undreaming, on a linen lap,
This, when the heart goes sick
And ears are threatened in the spring of dawn
By the triumphant accents of the cock,
Is more to be longed for in the end
Than, chained by syllables at hand and foot,
Wagging a wild tongue at the clock,
Deploring death, and raising roofs
Of words to keep unharmed
By time's approach in a fell wind
The bits and pieces of dissected loves.

February 1933 Notebook

In a letter to Trevor Hughes, the week this notebook was begun, Thomas defined 'what really makes you an artist': 'knowledge of the actual world's deplorable sordidness, and of the invisible world's splendour' (*Letters* p. 11). Thomas was explaining to his friend the vision which divides his poems into those of 'the outer, and absurd, world that changes' and those of 'true beauty ... which is undestroyable'. In the *February 1933 Notebook* we sense his striving for 'the inner splendour'; but, he admits, 'My poems rarely contain any of it. That is why they are not satisfactory to me. Most of them are the outer poems' (*Letters* p. 12).

'This Book Started February 1, 1933' – the heading heralds a new lease on life in the outer world. Thomas had left his newspaper job around the beginning of the year. He could now concentrate on his poetry; and, from the security of his home life in Swansea, he could begin to look to a literary career in London. Just that week he had read of a promising journal to be called *New Verse*; he soon submitted a batch of poems from his 'innumerable exercise books' (*Letters* p. 19). But the editor, Geoffrey Grigson, returned them. Success was not yet in Thomas's grasp. Indeed, the notebook begins on a morbid note: 'Companionship with night has turned/Each ugly corpse into a friend'. 'I continue writing', he tells Trevor Hughes in London, 'in the most futile manner, looking at the gas-oven' (*Letters* p. 14). But too much

123

is going on for him to stay depressed. He is active in Swansea Little Theatre, appearing in February as the Host in *Merry Wives of Windsor*, and in March as a principal in a modern comedy, *Peter and Paul*. In May 1933 he finally gets a poem into a London journal; *New English Weekly* prints "And death shall have no dominion." And then a poem he has submitted to a BBC Poetry Contest wins a reading on the National Service on 28 June 1933. To cap it all, he can spend the summer anticipating his first trip to London; he is invited to visit his newly married sister on a Thames houseboat.

The poems reflect the mutability of this 'outer' life. Then there are some, like "Find meat on bones" ("Forty Six"). that capture the inner splendour. Then, towards the end of the notebook, some poems seem to fulfil Thomas's aim of reconciling inner and outer.

One

Sweet as the comets' kiss night sealed
New faith, and dark the new friend fell,
With an ease and a smoothness I knew of old,
Irregular cries in the wind
Meaning no more than before, but with peace,
Peace of the grave, grave images,
Lending what wounded when light
Hurt the nerves and the heavy heart,
New light, grave light.

With night's coming was going,
Night's faces stared out the day's,
Smiles and white teeth giving place
To coldstone gazing through the ice,
Unchanging, unmoving, coldfrost.
Night's voices drowned the day's.

Companionship with night has turned
Each ugly corpse into a friend,
And there are more friends if you wish:
The maggots feasting on dead flesh,
The vulture with appraising beak,
The redcheeked vampire at the neck,
There is the skeleton and the naked ghost.
Friend of the night, you are friend of the night's friends.

Night's music crept through the tunnels
Of sleep, sleep of the grave, cracked passages,
Sounded fever of sounds soon dying,
Dark messages, terrors before waking,
Of the terrors of men, of men broken,
Maimed men and men killed by smiles,
By the lifting of Leah's hand
And the patient drooping of Rachel's head.

The fever passed, hot palms
Were cool again, touched by the night.

125

What were dreams between friends
Ran through sleep to dead ends,
Unwholesome thoughts struck sanitary checks,
Taut thoughts were lax,
Kind as a dog, the night,
Night of the grave, grave night,
Made its friends yours – the skeleton,
The eaten corpse, the black moth,
Symbols of peace and death –
For you are the night's friend,
Friend of the grave, grave friend.

February 1 1933.

Two

It is death though I have died
Many deaths, and have risen again
With an unhealed wound and a cracked heart,
It is death to sink again
My breath and blood into another
Who, too, has been wounded, has shown fight,
Has been killed, raised with a cracked heart
And is ready for the hundredth dying,
Ready to perish again and be hurt, is mad.
It is death to sink or to refuse,
Death either way.
Let me love then and let my old corpse lie
Among my other skeletons
Staring into the cracked sky.

February 2 '33.

Three

Had she not loved me at the beginning
There would have been no beginning,
Life in my mouth would not have tasted surely,
I would not have gone up to the places of the angels,
Seen heaven, known hell, known life turn in my mouth
From vinegar to sugar and then to vinegar again.
There would have been no beginning,
End would have come before the wind of heaven
Stirred, like a lizard, in my hair.
My hands would not have changed to snakes.

I planted a rose in her head.
I parted the serpents on her brow,
And drew the maggots from her breast.

Four

Before the gas fades with a harsh last bubble,
And the hunt in the hatstand discovers no coppers,
Before the last fag and the shirt sleeves and slippers,
The century's trap will have snapped round your middle,
Before the allotment is weeded and sown,
And the oakum is picked, and the spring trees have grown
           green,
And the state falls to bits,
And is fed to the cats,
Before civilization rises or rots
(It's a matter of guts,
Graft, poison, and bluff,
Sobstuff, mock reason,
The chameleon coats of the big bugs and shots),
The jaws will have shut, and life be switched out.
Before the arrival of angel or devil,

Before evil or good, light or dark,
Before white or black, the right or left sock,
Before good or bad luck.

Man's manmade sparetime lasts the four seasons,
Is empty in springtime, and no other time lessens
The bitter, the wicked, the longlying leisure,
Sleep punctured by waking, dreams
Broken by choking,
The hunger of living, the oven and gun
That turned on and lifted in anger
Make the hunger for living
When the purse is empty
And the belly is empty,
The harder to bear and the stronger.
The century's trap will have closed for good
About you, flesh will perish, and blood
Run down the world's gutters,
Before the world steadies, stops rocking, is steady,
Or rocks, swings and rocks, before the world totters.

Caught in the trap's machinery, lights out,
With sightless eyes and hearts that do not beat,
You will not see the steadying or falling,
Under the heavy layers of the night
Not black or white or left or right.

Feb 6, 33.

Five

Hold on, whatever slips beyond the edge,
To hope, a firefly in the veins; to trust
Of loving; to keeping close, lest
Words set septic, the loving thinking;
To what's unharmed by truths and lies, stays
Fixed fair in the brain, its closet shut
From wind and speech and this and that.

Was there a time when any fiddles,
Moaning in unison, could stop day troubles,
Start some new loving, cure ten aches?
There was a time I could cry over books.
But time has put its maggots on my track.

This laststraw hope, secure from blight,
And trust of loving what the seconds' germs
Have left unfouled, must never see the light.
Under the arc of the sky they are unsafe;
What's never known is safest in this life;
Under the skysigns you who have no arms
Have cleanest hands; out of the grave the ghost
Alone's unhurt, having no heart; you with no ears
Shall not be killed by words. And the blind man sees best.

Feb. 8. '33.

Six

After the funeral, mule praises, brays,
Shaking of mule heads betoken
Grief at the going to the earth of man
Or woman, at yet another long woe broken,
Another theme to play on and surprise
Fresh faults and till then hidden flaws
Faded beyond ears and eyes,

129

At him or her, loved or else hated well,
So far from love or hate in a deep hole.

The mourners in their Sabbath black
Drop tears unheeded or choke back a sob,
Join in the hymns, and mark with dry bright looks
The other heads, bent, spying, on black books.

Death has rewarded him or her for living,
With generous hands has slain with little pain,
And let the ancient face die with a smile.

Another gossips' toy has lost its use,
Broken lies buried amid broken toys,
Of flesh and bone lies hungry for the flies,
Waits for the natron and the mummy paint
With dead lips pursed and dry bright eyes;
Another well of rumours and cold lies
Has dried, and one more joke has lost its point.

Feb 10. '33.

Seven

'We who were young are old. It is the oldest cry.
Age sours before youth's tasted in the mouth
And any sweetness that it hath
Is sucked away'.

We who are still young are old. It is a dead cry,
The squeal of the damned out of the old pit.
We have grown weak before we could grow strong,
For us there is no shooting and no riding,
The Western man has lost one lung
And cannot mount a clotheshorse without bleeding.

Until the whisper of the last trump louden
We shall play Chopin in our summer garden,

With half-averted heads, as if to listen,
Play Patience in the parlour after dark.
For us there is no riding and no shooting,
No frosty gallops through the winter park.
We who are young sit holding yellow hands
Before the fire, and hearken to the wind.

Feb 16 '33

Eight

To take to give is all, return what given
Is throwing manna back to heaven,
Receive, not asking, and examine
Is looking gift god in the mouth.
To take to leave is pleasing death;
Unpleasant death will take at last,
Surrender at the very first
Is paying twice the final cost.

Nine

(Conclusion of Poem Seven)

No faith to fix the teeth on carries
Men old before their time into dark valleys
Where death lies dead asleep, one bright eye open,
No faith to sharpen the old wits leaves us
Lost in the shades, no course, no use
To fight through the invisible weeds,
No faith to follow is the world's curse
That falls on chaos.

There is but one message for the earth,
Young men with fallen chests and old men's breath,

131

Women with cancer at their sides
And cancerous speaking dripping from their mouths,
And lovers turning on the gas,
Exsoldiers with horrors for a face,
A pig's snout for a nose,
The lost in doubt, the nearly mad, the young
Who, undeserving, have suffered the earth's wrong,
The living dead left over from the war,
The living after, the filled with fear,
The caught in the cage, the broken winged,
The flying loose, albino eyed, wing singed,
The white, the black, the yellow and mulatto
From Harlem, Bedlam, Babel, and the Ghetto,
The Piccadilly men, the back street drunks,
The grafters of cats' heads on chickens' trunks,
The whole, the crippled, the weak and strong,
The Western man with one lung gone –
Faith fixed beyond the spinning stars,
Fixed faith, believing and worshipping together
In god or gods, christ or his father,
Mary, virgin, or any other.
Faith. Faith. Firm faith in many or one,
Faith fixed like a star beyond the stars,
And the skysigns and the night lights,
And the shores of the last sun.

We who are young are old, and unbelieving,
Sit at our hearths from morning until evening,
Warming dry hands and listening to the air;
We have no faith to set between our teeth.
Believe, believe and be saved, we cry, who have no faith.

Feb 17 '33.

Ten

Out of a war of wits, when folly of words
Was the world's to me, and syllables
Fell hard as whips on an old wound,
My brain came crying into the fresh light,
Called for confessor but there was none
To purge after the wits' fight,
And I was struck dumb by the sun.
Praise that my body be whole, I've limbs,
Not stumps, after the hour of battle,
For the body's brittle and the skin's white.
Praise that only the wits are hurt after the wits' fight.
The sun shines strong, dispels
Where men are men men's smells.
Overwhelmed by the sun, with a torn brain
I stand beneath the clouds' confessional,
But the hot beams rob me of speech,
After the perils of fools' talk
Reach asking arms up to the milky sky,
After a volley of questions and replies
Lift wit-hurt head for sun to sympathize,
And the sun heals, closing sore eyes.
It is good that the sun shine,
And, after it has sunk, the sane moon,
For out of a house of matchboard and stone
Where men would argue till the stars be green,
It is good to step onto the earth, alone,
And be struck dumb, if only for a time.

February 22 '33

Eleven

In wasting one drop from the heart's honey cells,
One precious drop that, for the moment, quells
Desire's pain, eases love's itch and ills,

133

There's less remains, for only once love fills,
When love's mouth knows its greatest thirst.
That great love, in its passion, demands all
The honey that man had at first
Before, unthinkingly, he shared its gold
With one and all, being love's child.
In those far days he was not very old
In love, knew little of love's wrong.
Wrong love took much, and when love's great mouth called,
In earnest from a woman's face,
Little there was to moisten of the honey hoard.

Feb 23 '33.

Twelve

With all the fever of the August months,
The winter convalescence,
In this damned world there's little to moan over
But the passing of the one and the coming of the other.
Lines of verse call out their echoes,
The lambs at teat with every rural note
Blown out of the tin-whistle,
Jerk infirm legs and patter little feet,
Goats describe a measure at the flute
Of every nature-writer from Fleet-street.
Though sucked year in year out
There's life in the earth's teat still.
What life in the pit of the soul?
Dry as an adder, it's a dark hole.
(Squeeze with the top of a cracked quill
Farts out of a dead mule.)

A crazy man, who might pass minutes
Of a bad day, when his thoughts slunk
Up all the blind ends, blind drunk,
In laughing fits at cul-de-sacs and sanities,
Might, in the dark, under the sheets' warmth,

134

Find some few things to cherish on the earth,
Under the layers of a mad mind
Perceive the gropings after love, and blind
As a mole, know not that what is cherished perishes.
With flowers to smell and fruits to eat,
He knows the horrible desires,
With winter passing and near heat
Of summer, knows the killings and cures
(Kill to stop what will be stopped,
And cure to delay).
With rags on the ragged bones and a bent hat
A crazy man might make some good
Out of a bad day.
The seasons are
Nothing more
Than hot and cold markings from one to four,
With little for a sane man to deplore
But the burning of one and the blowing of one more.

End of Feb. '33

Thirteen

Their faces shone under some radiance
Of mingled moonlight and lamplight
That turned the empty kisses into meaning,
The island of such penny love
Into a costly country, the graves
That neighboured them to wells of warmth
(And skeletons had sap). One minute
Their faces shone; the midnight rain
Hung pointed in the wind,
Before the moon shifted and the sap ran out,
She, in her summer frock, saying some cheap thing,
And he replying,
Not knowing radiance came and passed.
The suicides parade again, now ripe for dying.

Fourteen

I have longed to move away
From the hissing of the spent lie;
And the old terrors' continual cry
Growing more terrible as the day
Goes over the hill into the deep sea,
Night, careful of topography,
Climbs over the coal-tips where children play;
And the repetition of salutes
For ladies, the stale acts of the mutes;
And the thunder far off but not far enough
Of friendships turned to ghosts' hates
By telephone calls or notes,
For there are ghosts in the air
And ghostly echoes on paper;
I have longed to move but am afraid.

Some life, yet unspent, might explode
Out of the lie hissing on the ground
Like some sulphurous reminder of November,
And, cracking into the air, leave me half blind.
This must be avoided at all costs.
I would not care to die at the hands of ghosts,
Or lose my eyes through the last sparks of half lies.
Neither by night's ancient fear,
The parting of hat from hair,
Pursed lips at the receiver,
Shall I fall to death's feather.
The terror of night is a half terror,
Day no sharer of the black horror,
Out of the hours' span, half
Alone allowing the last thief
To breathe, stopping breath;
Salutation is a half convention
Regaining impoliteness when the hat's in position,
Half decorum kills what's left
Of the sane half no need to lift;
Then there is the sweet smile

And the snake's head grinning in the soul;
These are the smiles of night and day;
What I see is a half smile,
Half convention and half lie;
By these I would not care to die.

March 1 '33

Sixteen

The waking in a single bed when light
Fell on the upturned oval of her face
And morning's sun shone vast in the sky
(Her last night's lover) is gone forever,
Her legal honour sold to one man for good
Who will disturb the rhythms of her blood.
Where there was one are two, and nothing's shared
Of love and light in all this spinning world
Save the love-light of half love smeared
Over the countenance of the two-backed beast
Which nothing knows of rest but lust
And lust, love knows, soon perishes the breast,
Reducing the rose, for want of a lovelier
Image on the ghost of paper,
Of single love to dust.

No longer with its touch kind as a mother's
Will the vibrations of day settle on
The pillow in pale lights where once she lay alone,
Heart hardly beating under its frame of ribs,
Lips catching the honey of the golden
Sun small as a farthing
Hiding behind a cloud, for where
She lies another lies at her side,
And through his circling arm she feels
The secret coursing of his blood
Filling her fingers with a hundred pins
Each sharper than the last.

And the moon-ghost no longer
Will come as a stranger in the night
Filling her head with moon's light.

Two lay where one lay lover for the sun.
Death, last lover, is the lover to come.
Who, warm-veined, can love another
Mortal thing as an immortal lover?
No moon or sun, two taking one's couch,
Will shine the same, love each
As once he loved her who had one name.

It can be called a sacrifice. It can
With equal truth under the vast sun
Be called the turning of sun's love to man,
And now in the cold night
There can be no warming by sun's light.

March 22 '33.

Seventeen

See, on gravel paths under the harpstrung trees,
He steps so near the water that a swan's wing
Might play upon his lank locks with its wind,
The lake's voice and the rolling of mock waves
Make discord with the voice within his ribs
That thunders as heart thunders, slows as heart slows.
Is not his heart imprisoned by the summer
Snaring the whistles of the birds
And fastening in its cage the flowers' colour?
No, he's a stranger, outside the season's humour,
Moves, among men caught by the sun,
With heart unlocked upon the gigantic earth.
He alone is free, and, free, moans to the sky.
He, too, could touch the season's lips and smile,
Under the hanging branches hear the winds' harps.
But he is left. Summer to him

138

Is the ripening of apples,
The unbosoming of the sun,
And a delicate confusion in the blood.

So shall he step till summer loosens its hold
On the canvas sky, and all hot colours melt
Into the browns of autumn and the sharp whites of winter,
And so complain, in a vain voice, to the stars.

Even among his own kin is he lost,
Is love a shadow on the wall,
Among all living men is a sad ghost.
He is not man's nor woman's man,
Leper among a clean people
Walks with the hills for company,
And has the mad trees' talk by heart.

There is no place, no woman bares her breasts
For him to lay his head, weary with images, in the valley
Between the breasts, no silver girl
Offers her body to him as a lover
Offers her silver body; he is no lover,
And though he battle against the skies
And the stars is no warrior.

An image of decay disturbs the crocus
Opening its iris mouth upon the sill
Where fifty flowers breed in a fruit box,
And washing water spilt upon their necks
Cools any ardour they may have
And he destroys, though flowers are his loves,
If love he can being no woman's man.
An image born out of the uproarious spring
Hastens the time of the geranium to breathe;
Life, till the change of mood, forks
From the unwatered leaves and the stiff stalks,
The old flowers' legs too taut to dance,
But he makes them dance, cut capers
Choreographed on paper.

The image changes, and the flowers drop
Into their prison with a slack sound,
Fresh images surround the tremendous moon,
Or catch all death that's in the air –
Whether from passing smiles set on stale lips,
The deadly rain that strikes the slates,
The bloated dogs floating upon the river.

O lonely among many, the gods' man,
Knowing exceeding grief and the gods' sorrow
That, like a razor, skims, cuts, and turns,
Aches till the metal meets the marrow,
You, too, know the exceeding joy
And the triumphant crow of laughter.
Out of a bird's wing writing on a cloud
You capture more than man or woman guesses;
Rarer delight shoots in the blood
At the deft movements of the irises
Growing in public places than man knows;
There in the sunset and sunrise
Joy lifts its head, wonderful with surprise.
A rarer wonder is than man supposes.

See, on gravel paths under the harpstrung trees,
Feeling the summer wind, hearing the swans,
Leaning from windows over a length of lawns,
On level hills admiring the sea
Or the steeples of old towns
Stabbing the changing sky, he is alone,
Alone complains to the stars.
Who are his friends? The wind is his friend,
The glow-worm lights his darkness, and
The snail tells of coming rain.

Poem completed March 31 '33.

Eighteen

Make me a mask to shut from razor glances
Of men's eyes and the stare of day
Rape and rebellion on my face,
A countenance hewed out of river ice,
Glass image that with no glance compromises,
Or wooden with uncompromising lenses
To let my own edged eyes perceive
Others betraying the inner love or lie
By the curve of the mouth or the laugh up the sleeve.
Graft on me a perpetually untwinkling smile,
A slit from ear to ear on ice or glass
Deceiving each pretty miss who passing
Smiles back confessing a treacherous heart,
Unlicensed promise under a cheap skirt,
Bee's sting under her mask of paint.

A snake, charmed by the sketching of two hands
In lunatic gestures on the market air
Or rank breath in the booths of a bazaar,
Hissed the little circle of its mouth,
Feeling some music rub against its senses,
And, to the pipe, wriggled the wet length of its tail,
Lifting two cold eyes to catch men's glances.
There is an old evil in the snake's dancing,
But where it lies passes men's guesses
Which cannot probe the evil of the dark
Slaying daylight and turning the wind sick.
There is an old evil in the snake's eyes,
Two black circles squeezed in a squat head.
Its eyes see nothing, are stone-cold and dead.
The mouth hissed, quick to kill. Men cannot tell
The evil in those two stones in the sun,
Or glimpse the wickedness in that wet mask.

Make *me* a mask to wall away
My face from the face of day
And the colloquial stare that tears in six

141

The inner love or lie, the eyes of snakes
Themselves envisored from men's looks,
The loop-holes of the spying houses
Picking from virtues a live nest of vices,
The sly vermin and the grimaces
Of men whose smiles were stamped upon their faces
By furrows of the black plague or the pox.

Nineteen

To follow the fox at the hounds' tails
And at their baying move a tailor's inch
To follow, wild as the chicken stealer,
Scent through the clutches of the heather,
Leads to fool's paradise where the redcoated killer
Deserves no brush, but a fool's ambush,
Broken flank or head-on crash.
Following the nose down dell, up rise
Into the map-backed hills where paths
Cross all directions, bracken points to the skies,
Leads, too, to a lead pit, whinny and fall,
No fox, no good, fool's, not a fox's, hole,
And that is the reward of labour
Through heath and heather at the mind's will.
To follow the nose if the nose goes
Wisely at the dogs' tails, leads
Through easier heather to the foul lair
Over a road thick with the bones of words.
If hunting means anything more than the chase
On a mare's back of a mare's nest or a goose,
Then only over corpses shall the feet tread,
Crunching the already broken, breaking
Butt-ends lying at dead-ends forsaken,
And this way leads to good and bed,
Where more than snails are friends,

There is a smell that carries glamour
Into the nostrils, man's blooded by Diana,
Or by a clean, not hare-lipped, god.

March 28 '32

Twenty

The ploughman's gone, the hansom driver,
Left in the records of living a not-to-be-broken picture,
In sun and rain working for good and gain,
Left only the voice in the old village choir
To remember, cast stricture on mechanics and man.
The windmills of the world still stand
With wooden arms revolving in the wind
Against the rusty sword and the old horse
Bony and spavined, rich with fleas.
But the horses are gone and the reins are green
As the hands that held them in my father's time.
The wireless snarls on the hearth.
Beneath a balcony the pianola plays
Black music to a Juliet in her stays
Who lights a fag-end at the flame of love.
No more toils over the fields
The rawboned horse to a man's voice
Telling it this, patting its black nose:
You shall go as the others have gone,
Lay your head on a hard bed of stone,
And have the raven for companion.
The ploughman's gone, the hansom driver,
With rain-beaten hands holding the whip,
Masters over unmastered nature,
Soil's stock, street's stock, of the moon lit, ill lit, field and town,
Lie cold, with their horses, for raven and kite.

Man toils now on an iron saddle, riding
In sun and rain over the dry shires,
Hearing the engines, and the wheat dying.

Sometimes at his ear the engine's voice
Revolves over and over again
The same tune as in my father's time:
You shall go as the others have gone,
Lay your head on a hard bed of stone,
And have the raven for companion.
It is the engine and not the raven.
Man who once drove is driven in sun and rain.
It is the engine for companion.
It is the engine under the unaltered sun.

March 28 '33

Twenty One

Light, I know, treads the ten million stars,
And blooms in the Hesperides. Light stirs
Out of the heavenly sea onto the moon's shores.
Such light shall not illuminate my fears
And catch a turnip ghost in every cranny.
I have been frightened of the dark for years.
When the sun falls and the moon stares,
My heart hurls from my side and tears
Drip from my open eyes as honey
Drips from the humming darkness of the hive.
I am a timid child when light is dead.
Unless I learn the night I shall go mad.
It is night's terrors I must learn to love,
Or pray for day to some attentive god
Who on his cloud hears all my wishes,
Hears and refuses.
Light walks the sky, leaving no print,
And there is always day, the shining of some sun,
In those high globes I cannot count,
And some shine for a second and are gone,
Leaving no print.
But lunar light will not glow in my blackness,
Make bright its corners where a skeleton

Sits back and smiles, a tiny corpse
Turns to the roof a hideous grimace,
Or mice play with an ivory tooth.
Stars' light and sun's light will not shine
As clearly as the light of my own brain,
Will only dim life, and light death.
I must learn night's light or go mad.

April 1 '33

Twenty Two

My body knows its wants that, often high
As a high cloud attendant on the sun,
Or small as the small globes of the dew,
Defy the trying of a host of men
Who cannot satisfy, might satisfy the sky
As easily, or cut the moon in two.
Men want the stars to hang on cherry trees,
Drop, with a fruit's sound, at their shoes,
And the fantastic circle of the sun,
Will never rest, being mad men,
Until they dam and turn the lunar lake
Behind the railings of a private park,
And graft the mad plants of the moon
On to the green arbutus grown at home.
But, though they reach, they cannot touch and take
Sun, moon, and stars, to be their own.
These they cannot compass in their thoughts,
Nor can they spangle the miles of city streets
With the globes of the dew and the celestial lights.

Finding new friends you breed new wants;
A friend is but an enemy on stilts
Striding so high above the common earth
Where war moves not the planets in their course
An inch more than armistice, signed with a cross,
You cannot see his eyes or know his faults.

145

Man's wants remain unsatisfied till death.
Then, when his soul is naked, is he one
With the man in the wind, and the west moon,
With the harmonious thunder of the sun.

April 2. '33

Twenty Three

And death shall have no dominion.
Man, with soul naked, shall be one
With the man in the wind and the west moon,
With the harmonious thunder of the sun;
When his bones are picked clean and the clean bones gone,
He shall have stars at elbow and foot;
Though he fall mad he shall be sane,
And though he drown he shall rise up again;
Though lovers be lost, love shall not;
And death shall have no dominion.

And death shall have no dominion.
Under green shiftings of the sea
Man shall lie long but shall not die,
And under the white darkness of the snow;
Twisting on racks when sinews give way,
Strapped to a wheel, yet he shall not break;
Faith, in his hands, shall snap in two,
And all the swords of evil run him through;
Split all ends up, he shan't crack;
And death shall have no dominion.

And death shall have no dominion.
No more may gulls cry at his ear,
Or waves break loud on the sea shore,
Telling some wonder to the salty air;
Where blew a flower may a flower no more
Lift its head to the blows of the rain;
Beauty may vanish at his stare,

And, when he shield his eyes, again be fair;
Beauty may blossom in pain;
And death shall have no dominion.

And death shall have no dominion.
Under the sea or snow at last
Man shall discover all he thought lost,
And hold his little soul within his fist;
Knowing that now can he never be dust,
He waits in the sun till the sun goes out;
Now he knows what he had but guessed
Of living and dying and all the rest;
He knows his soul. There is no doubt.
And death shall have no dominion.

April '33

Twenty Four

Within his head revolved a little world
Where wheels, confusing music, confused doubts,
Rolled down all images into the pits
Where half dead vanities were sleeping curled
Like cats, and lusts lay half hot in the cold.

Within his head the engines made their hell,
The veins at either temple whipped him mad,
And, mad, he called his curses upon God,
Spied moon-mad beasts carousing on the hill,
Mad birds in trees, and mad fish in a pool.
Across the sun was spread a crazy smile.
The moon leered down the valley like a fool.

Now did the softest sound of foot or voice
Echo a hundred times, the flight of birds
Drum harshly on the air, the lightning swords

Tear with a great sound through the skies,
And there was thunder in an opening rose.

All reason broke, and horror walked the roads.
A smile let loose a devil, a bell struck.
He could hear women breathing in the dark,
See women's faces under living snoods,
With serpents' mouths and scolecophidian voids
Where eyes should be, and nostrils full of toads.

Taxis and lilies to tinned music stept
A measure on the lawn where cupids blew
Water through every hole, a Sanger's show
Paraded up the aisles and in the crypt
Of churches made from abstract and concrete.
Pole-sitting girls descended for a meal,
Stopped non-stop dancing to let hot feet cool,
Or all-in wrestling for torn limbs to heal,
The moon leered down the valley like a fool.

Where, what's my God among this crazy rattling
Of knives on forks, he cried, of nerve on nerve,
Man's ribs on woman's, straight line on a curve,
And hand to buttock, man to engine, battling,
Bruising, where's God's my Shepherd, God is Love?
No loving shepherd in this upside life.

So crying, he was dragged into the sewer,
Voles at his armpits, down the sad canal
Where floated a dead dog who made him ill,
Plunged in black waters, under hail and fire,
Knee-deep in vomit. I saw him there,
And thus I saw him searching for his soul.

And swimming down the gutters he looks up
At cotton worlds revolving on a hip,
Riding on girders of the air, looks down
On garages and clinics in the town.

Where, what's my God among this taxi stepping,

This lily crawling round the local pubs?
It was November there were whizzbangs hopping,
But now there are the butt-ends of spent squibs.

So crying, he was pushed into the Jordan.
He, too, has known the agony in the Garden,
And felt a skewer enter at his side.
He, too, has seen the world as bottom rotten,
Kicked, with a clatter, ash-bins marked verboten,
And heard the teeth of weasels drawing blood.

And thus I saw him. He was poised like this,
One hand at head, the other at a loss,
Between the street-lamps and the ill-lit sky,
And thus, between the seasons, heard him cry:

Where, what's my God? I have been mad, am mad,
Have searched for shells and signs on the sea shore,
Stuck straw and seven stars upon my hair,
And leant on stiles and on the golden bar,
I have ridden on gutter dung and cloud.
Under a hideous sea where coral men
Feed in the armpits of drowned girls, I've swum
And sunk; waved flags to every fife and drum;
Said all the usual things over and again;
Lain with parched things; loved dogs and women;
I have desired the circle of the sun.
Tested by fire, double thumb to nose,
I've mocked the moving of the universe.
Where, what? There was commotion in the skies,
But no god rose. I have seen bad and worse,
Gibed the coitus of the stars. No god
Comes from my evil or my good. Mad, mad,
Feeling the pinpricks of the blood, I've said
The novel things. But it has been no good.

Crying such words, he left the crying crowds,
Unshackled the weights of words from tired limbs,
And took to feeding birds with broken crumbs

149

Of old divinities, split bits of names.
Very alone, he ploughed the only way.
And thus I saw him in a square of fields,
Knocking off turnip tops, with trees for friends,
And thus, some time later, I heard him say:

Out of the buildings of the day I've stept
To hermits' huts, and talked to ancient men.
Out of the noise into quiet I ran.
My God's a shepherd, God's the love I hoped.
The moon peers down the valley like a saint.
Taxis and lilies, noise and no noise,
Pair off, make harmonies, harmonious chord,
For he has found his soul in loneliness,
Now he is one with many, one with all,
Fire and Jordan and the sad canal.
Now he has heard and read the happy word.
Still, in his hut, he broods among his birds.
I see him in the crowds, not shut
From you or me or wind or rat
Or this or that.

Started April 16 '33
Completed April 20 '33

Twenty Five

Not from this anger, anticlimax after
Refusal struck her face, a clap of laughter,
And smiles sucked out the humour from her offer,
Shall she receive a bellyful of stones,
Nor from surprise at what turned out
Wrong choice, later, in the hotkneed night,
Shall sin amuse her limbs, and hands
Leap over the barbed lands.
For she made no adjustment to how men

150

React to offers of a home for semen,
Refused to fit the voice of passion
Into men's laughs and smiles set in position,
So felt passion and reaction not at all
But lay, not deflowered, on a lily bed,
Lilies reposing in the cool
Of pit and limb, a lily for a lad.

Behind my head a square of sky sags over
The smile tossed from lover to lover,
And the golden ball shines in another.
Among the couples, I sit and mark
Love wet its arrow in the park.
Combinations, operations, generations.
There's the same cry in friction and pistons,
In the voice of engines churning
Butter from milk, the same questions.
Love has only one turning.
Why, then, the lowroads and high roads,
Byroads to no roads? Shall it matter
If anger or laughter or letter
Leads from hauteur to offer? Take
What is offered before it break.

Not from this anger, anticlimax after
Refusal struck her face, shall I
Be one with many under the sagging sky,
With Harry and Gladys and Herbert and May,
And all the others who lie,
Cats in a basket, catching the moment's honey.
There should be no surprise, wrong choice;
Two are as good as one
Under the spinning circle of the sun;
A bad one's better than one,
Says the daisy's, the engine's, voice.

April 20 '33

Twenty Six

The first ten years in school and park
Leapt like a ball from light to dark,
Bogies scared from landing and from corner,
Leapt on the bed, but now I've sterner
Stuff inside, dole for no work's
No turnip ghost now I'm no minor.
Dead are the days of thumbstained primer,
Outpourings of old soaks in censored books;
Brother spare a dime sounds louder
Than the academicians' thunder; sooner
Be fed with food than dreams. Still,
There was sense in Harrow on the Hill,
The playing fields of Eton, matchboard huts
Where youths learnt more than cigarettes and sluts,
Or on the coal tips near the engines
Where children played at Indians, scalps
Littered the raven Alps. There was meaning in this.
The next five years from morn to even
Hung between hell and heaven,
Plumbed devil's depths, reached angel's heights;
Dreams would have tempted saints at nights;
Night after night I climbed to bed,
The same thoughts in my head.
The last five years passed at a loss,
Fitting, all vainly, hopes dead as mown grass,
Fire and water of my young nonsense,
Height and depth, into the modern synthesis.
There were five years of trying
Mingling of living and dying.
So much of old and new, the old and new
Out of the war to make another,
Past and present, would not fit together,
And I, as you, was caught between
The field and the machine.
What was there to make of birds'
And factory's whistles but discords?
No music in the dynamo and harp.

152

Five years found no hope
Of harmony, no cure, till this year,
For bridging white and black,
The left and right sock, light and dark,
Pansy and piston, klaxon horn
And owl addressing moon.

Until you learn the keyboard, keys,
Struck down together, make harsh noise.
Follow this best of recipes.

Tune in to a tin organ at Toulouse,
Or in Appreciation Hour, run by the States,
Let pinches of tinned Mozart please,
Never forget, when hearing Bach on flutes,
Or after-dinner symphonies, that lots
Of people like that sound of noise,
Let cataracts of sound fall on your ears,
Listen in pain, till pain agrees.

That music understood, then there's another:
The music of turbine and lawn mower,
Hard, soft headed ecstasy,
Of plough and Ford along the earth,
Blackbird and Blue Bird, moth and Moth.

So much of old and new, the old and new
Out of the war to make another,
Past and present, will fit together
When the keys are no mysteries.
Twenty years; and now this year
Has found a cure.
New music, from new and loud, sounds on the air.

April 22 '33

Twenty Seven

Pass through twelve stages, reach the fifth
By retrograde moving from near death,
And puberty recoils at callow youth
Knowing such stuff as will confuse
That phantom in the blood, used to misuse,
Red rims, a little learning, and calf sense.
In carpet slippers, with a broken crutch,
Retrogress from pitch to pitch,
Leave the oncoming shadow at the door,
Leave it your odd shoes.
Let the scales fall from rheumy eyes,
And, stepping back through medium of abuse,
Excess or otherwise, regain your fire.
Graft a monkey gland, old man, at fools' advice.

Shall it be male or female? say the cells.
The womb deliberates, spits forth manchild
To break or to be broken by the world,
A body cursed already by heredity.
The hundred-tainted lies in the cold and cools.

A one-legged man ascending steps
Looks down upon him with regrets
That whips and stools and cistern sex
Have yet to add to that that mother strips
Upon her knee and shields from metal whisper
Of wind along the cot,
Sees cool get cold and childmind darker
As time on time sea ribbon rounds
Parched shires in dry lands.

The hundred-tainted must pulse and grow,
Victim of sires' vices breed heirs
To herring smelling fevers,
By way of ditch and gap arrive full stop.

Old man, would you arrive at pain,

Although new pain, by back lane,
Not dodging ruts but stepping through them,
Soaking old legs and veins,
And reach your youth again by them.

The child on lap is a nice child,
Has learnt, through cold, to love the heat,
On female knees takes a warm seat,
And this is all there is to it:
The victim of grandfather's
Or even earlier's unwise desires
Has a hundred stigmas,
More chance to hand on
Unclean Round Robin,
And more to hear air engine,
May yet find wings as airman,
And parachute old scabs and branded spots.

April 23 '33

Twenty Eight

First there was the lamb on knocking knees,
The ousel and the maniac greens of spring;
I caught on yard of canvas inch of wing,
Kingfisher's, gull's swooping feather and bone,
Goodnight and goodmorning of moon and sun;
First there was the lamb which grew a sheep.

There along the spring sky deep with milk
I chanced upon a vision in surprise;
I caught the selfsame vision treading trees,
A season's fancy flown into a figure;
First there was the spring lamb which grew bigger;
I saw the vision at the last moon's lip

Kiss and be answered: Spring fell spent on summer;
I heard the season's corpses in wind's walk

155

Talk with the voices of scissors through silk;
One sentence was spelt to me
By the typewriter ribbon of sea:
First there was the young man who grew old.

Summer spent spring's hoard, fell spent on winter;
Brown in the clouds rose autumn's rumour,
A season's fancy formed into a tumour;
The lamb grown sheep had lambs around its belly,
And teats like turnips for the lambs to bully;
First there was a body which grew cold.

First there was the boy, young man, and lover;
Love's face, he dared not think, would taint and tatter;
First love brought forth a fullvoiced litter,
A knock-kneed calf pulled at the navel string;
First love, calf love, is seldom wrong;
First there was the calf which grew a cow.

The seasons parturate; spring begets summer,
And summer autumn; autumn begets another,
The black sheep, shuffling of the fold, old winter;
And love's first litter begets more.
First there was innocence and then desire,
A maggot in the veins; there's nothing now.

There's nothing but the lamb on knocking knees,
The season's vision treading clouds and trees,
The ousel and the maniac greens of spring;
All this goes on for ever and too long;
I catch on a yard of canvas inch of wing.

May 13. '33

Twenty Nine

We lying by seasand watching yellow
And the grave sea, mock who deride
Who follow the red rivers, hollow
Alcove of words out of cicada shade,
Navy blue bellies of the tribes,
For in this yellow grave twixt sea and sand
A calling for colour calls with the wind
That's grave and grey as grave and sea
Supine on either hand.
Bound by the yellow strip, we lie,
Watch yellow, wish for wind to blow away
The strata of the shore and leave red rock.
But wishes breed not, neither
Can we fend off the sandy smother,
Nor tear the spindwind from our breath,
The seaweed from our chests,
Lie, watching yellow, until the yellow mists
Proclaim the last smother of death.

May 16 '33.

Thirty

Before We Sinned

Incarnate devil in a talking snake,
When god incarnate walked the garden,
Some sunless time when we were half awake,
Proffered in wind and leaf forbidden fruits,
Spoke evil with its scales.
And god walked cool, the ghostly warden,
And proffered pardon in the ghostly notes
His robe plucked from the hills.

We touched our hands upon a blade of grass;
One evil edge stung deep and bitter,

While from the other stole the sweetest juice
That, falling on our wounds, soon made them better.

When storm noised in the trees, unrisen stars
And the half moon halfhiding in the clouds
Talked good and evil till a world of fears
Grew sick around us, and made foul our words.
And when the moon came out, it was
Half white as wool, half green as grass.
And when the stars crept breathing from their shrouds,
Half were sweet signs, and half were scars.

We in our eden knew the ghostly warden
In crystal waters that no frost could harden
Nor any heat turn tepid in the mouth,
In treeroots tunnelling beneath the earth,
And knew that he and evil both
Spoke in the wind that tumbled from the north.

For unroused senses there were pepper trees;
Sharp lemons cured the twitching of the knees;
Knowing a cause and cure,
We knew the good and evil in desire.

Before we sinned we knew all evil,
Hearing in snow that turned to ice
The sibilant horror of the devil's voice,
And in the mutterings of the birds.
Before we sinned we heard god's words,
Condemning and then pardoning. Before we sinned.
Before we sinned was evil in the wind.

May 16 '33

Thirty One

Now understand a state of being, heaven
A state of being unbound by traitor senses,
Transforming to a thought that shapes it,
Ready for him who hates or rapes it,
Cool as ice, hot as an oven;
Now understand the fallacy of fancies
That gave god whiskers to his navel,
A tail and two horns to the devil.

Now understand a state of being, nothing
A state of being; future, past, and present;
Now understand the heaven prayed for
By men heaven was not made for,
By deacons out of a church coffin,
Is true to every detail and most pleasant;
Angels are there, and harps to strum on;
All things are upperclass, not common.

Now understand a state of being, future
A state of being, and present is soon past;
Each is a state in some set country
Explored by gangsters and the gentry,
Tinker, tailor, king, and preacher,
All who will find their paradise a frost,
And in eternal state of being
Wish for the nevergift of dying.

Now understand a state of being,
Reason for understanding these
Black words two eyes are seeing,
For being, reason, words and eyes.
Now understand a state of being.

May 18 '33.

Thirty Two

Interrogating smile has spoken death
To every day since I lay dumb
Upon a black lap in a swaddling cloth,
Pierced me with pain another knew
Who, once, a million days ago,
Longed for the tomb, bled like a lamb,
And knew forsaken horror on the tree.

A lifted arm has sketched a world enough
To fill with life ten times by mortal time,
And there has been a kingdom in a laugh.
But arm and lifted laugh have spoken doom,
Said acid things that burnt an hour in half,
Or split a foul day into three.

A footfall has its moon and sun,
A single syllable its many words;
Within the first note of a nursery tune,
A lifted laugh out of the flute,
There sound a heavenly host of chords.
What need I hear more than a single note,
Of what more than a single fist of clouds
That threatens and that never strikes need write?

A drop of water is both kind and cruel.
These worlds of foot and hand, of laugh and smile,
Hold every joy. Smile pierces quick to kill,
Smile eases. Here in this deep water all
Pain and all ease lie wonderful.
Here in this hesitating foot
Lies more of all than all the years can tell.

May 20 '33

Thirty Three

No man believes who, when a star falls shot,
Cries not aloud blind as a bat,
Cries not in terror when a bird is drawn
Into the quicksand feathers down,
Who does not make a wound in faith
When any light goes out, and life is death.

No man believes who cries not, god is not,
Who feels not coldness in the heat,
In the breasted summer longs not for spring,
No breasted girl, no man who, young
And green, sneers not at the old sky.
No man believes who does not wonder why.

Believe and be saved. No man believes
Who curses not what makes and saves,
No man upon this cyst of earth
Believes who does not lance his faith,
No man, no man, no man.

And this is true, no man can live
Who does not bury god in a deep grave
And then raise up the skeleton again,
No man who does not break and make,
Who in the bones finds not new faith,
Lends not flesh to ribs and neck,
Who does not break and make his final faith.

May 23 '33

Thirty Five

Children's Song

When I lie in my bed and the moon lies in hers,
And when neither of us can sleep
For the brotherly wind and the noise of the stars,
And the motherless cries of the sheep,
I think of a night when the owl is still
And the moon is hid and the stars are dim,
And that is the night that death will call,
And the night that I most fear him.
Let the owl hoot and the sheep complain;
Let the brotherly wind speak low;
Death shall not enter in west wind and rain,
Let the wind blow.

July 1. '33. For P.T.

Thirty Six

The tombstone tells how she died.
She wed on a wild March morning;
Before she lay on her wedding bed
She died, was death's bride.
The tombstone tells how she died.
She married on a mad Welsh morning,
With March flowers over her head,
A farmer up valley who needed a girl
To sleep with and talk with, milk and clean sheds.
She died in her white wedding dress,
With a garland of roses, a Catholic cross,
A cake, and a ring, and a mirror inside
That showed death coming in.
The tombstone tells how she died.

July '33

Thirty Seven

Why east wind chills and south wind cools
Shall not be known till windwell dries
And west's no longer drowned
In winds that bring the fruit and rind
Of many a hundred falls.
Why grass is sweet and thistles prick,
And nighttime rain and mother's milk
Both quench his hourly thirst,
The fool shall question till he drop;
And till the mother mare at last
Lies on her bed, the colt at her dry pap
Nosing and wondering at dead flesh,
She shall have no reply.
Manure the field, and manure the field;
Isinglass, pelt, and ash;
And snow shall be fresh and dust be harsh,
And a whip cut weal and a spur draw blood.
What colour is glory? the children ask.
Shall they clasp a comet in their fists?
When cometh Jack Frost?

Not till, from high and low, their dust
Sprinkles in children's eyes a longlast sleep,
And dusk is crowded with the children's ghosts,
Shall there be answer and the world be lost
Where once a vulture with a naked neck
Caught up a lamb who watered at the brink,
Felt sweetness round the hollow of its tongue
And talons on its back.
Not till the moon falls from its place
Shall I know why the trees are dumb,
Or, in my innocence, know their mild voice;
Not till the worms feed at my face,
Shall there be answer, and the brain find silence.

What colour is glory? the children ask.
Shall they clasp a comet in their fists?

When cometh Jack Frost?

All things are known. The stars' advice
Calls some content to travel with the winds
Around the head where many questions meet.
Though what the stars say on their business
Of rounding time on time the shires of sky
Is heard but little till the stars go out.
I hear content, and, Be content,
Ring through the country of the air,
And, Walk content, and walk content
Though famine strips the valley big with war,
And, Know no answer, and I know
No answer to the children's ghostly cry
Of glory's colour, and the man of frost,
And ghostly comets over the raised fists.

July 1. *33*

Thirty Eight

This is remembered when the hairs drop out:
Love, like a stone, that struck and hurt;
And promise in the night.
When rheum around the eyes blinds sight
This is remembered: the winy wood
Where a wild pig sprang on its mate;
The smelling of roses; the first cigarette;
The first womb; the brain is heir to
The first attacking shot.
You'll remember appendix, a souvenir slit;
The preacher's buzz, communion blood;
A promise to a mother, if you care to;
A drunk, a head in the abbey;
There's a text and a photo, a garter, a drunk,
And a fair face you half forgot.
This is remembered when the veins are scrubby,
And the shellholed gums no longer pink.

What's not remembered is the way of walking;
Wood and no trees where wooden scorpion
Measured its scales' bisector;
Dreams' gall and nectar;
What's not remembered is half the mortal lecture.
(Who lectures but old God, a phantom rector,
A walking bible printed polyglot.)

Half is forgotten since your mother's milking,
And half the span of threescore years and ten;
Wind and no noise, walk and no stepping,
Wood and no trees, round half the rim of man.
Remember sleep; half metaphrase the circus,
And catch death like a trickhorse at your whip;
On sleep's sector of your sixty span
Walk, with no stepping, and surprise the plan.
The purpose shines along your trembling lip
That trembles with a snore. In the beginning
Was the word, the word began
In sleep no clock or calendar could time.

Half is remembered since your halfhands' knocking,
And ten teredo fingers bored the womb.

July 4 & 5. 33

Thirty Nine

In me ten paradoxes make one truth,
Ten twining roots meet twining in the earth
To make one root that never strangles light
By thrusting a green shrub from underneath;
And never shall the truth translate
From epileptic whispering in the night,
And never shall the roots bear to bear fruit
Till life and death shall cancel out,
First and last paradox are cancelled out.

As I am man, this paradox insists:

I am the one man living among ghosts,
The one ghost among men; I am the chosen
One, the one neglected in two mists.
In me man and woman's brazen,
Yet have I played the eunuch to all passion,
Having no sex and every feeling frozen.
Till life is death there'll be no reason,
Till life and death unite there'll be no reason.

July 33

Forty

(After the performance of Sophocles'
Electra in a garden.
Written for a local paper).

A woman wails her dead among the trees,
Under the green roof grieves the living;
The living sun laments the dying skies,
Lamenting falls. Pity Electra's loving

Of all Orestes' continent of pride
Dust in the little country of an urn,
Of Agamemnon and his kingly blood
That cries along her veins. No sun or moon

Shall lamp the raven darkness of her face,
And no Aegean wind cool her cracked heart;
There are no seacaves deeper than her eyes;
Day treads the trees and she the cavernous night.

Among the trees the language of the dead
Sounds, rich with life, out of a painted mask;
The queen is slain; Orestes' hands drip blood;
And women talk of horror to the dusk.

There can be few tears left: Electra wept
A country's tears and voiced a world's despair
At flesh that perishes and blood that's spilt
And love that goes down like a flower.

Pity the living who are lost, alone;
The dead in Hades have their host of friends,
The dead queen walketh with Mycenae's king
Through Hades' groves and the Eternal Lands.

Pity Electra loveless, she whose grief
Drowns and is drowned, who utters to the stars
Her syllables, and to the gods her love;
Pity the poor unpitied who are strange with tears.

Among the garden trees a pigeon calls,
And knows no woe that these sad players mouth
Of evil oracles and funeral ills;
A pigeon calls and women talk of death.

July 7. 33

Forty One

Praise to the architects;
Dramatic shadows in a tin box;
Nonstop; stoppress; vinegar from wisecracks;
Praise to the architects;
Radio's a building in the air;
The poster is today's text,
The message comes from negro mystics,
An old chatterbox, barenaveled at Nice,
Who steps on the gas;
Praise to the architects;
A pome's a building on a page;
Keatings is good for lice,
A pinch of Auden is the lion's feast;
Praise to the architects;

Empty, To Let, are signs on this new house;
To leave it empty's lion's or louse's choice;
Lion or louse? Take your own advice;
Praise to the architects.

July 7. '33

Forty Two

Here in this spring, stars float along the void,
Tealeaves on curd;
Here in this mothernaked winter
Down pelts the naked weather;
This summer buries a spring bird.

Symbols are selected from the years'
Slow rounding of four seasons' coasts,
In autumn teach three seasons' fires
And four birds' notes.
From symbols I know four in one,
The holy three from any fact or figure,
Christ from an ass's cross,
God from its bray, Ghost from its halter.

I should know summer from the trees, the worms
Tell, if tell at all, the winter's storms
Or the funeral of the sun;
I should tell spring by the cuckooing,
And the slug should say me destruction;
A worm tells summer better than the clock,
The slug's a living calendar of days.
What shall it teach me if a summer bug
Tell me spring wears away?
This: that a symbol's spring and summer;
I have the seasons' germs about my blood
That itch to action when a season's rumour,
In man or midge, is got and understood.
More than a bloody heart beats at my side;

A stone, a water's drop, behind the ribs
Lie living close; I have a stable god
In stall, heart's fodder, and will's whip.

July 9 '33

Forty Three

A praise of acid or a chemist's lotion
Waiting and willing on an elbow rest,
Resound and stick a needle of vibration
Through death's wax!
A hymn of ether and a surgeon's mask,
A fencer's edge dependent on the thumbs,
Follow the leaden echo of a coward's task,
Tap death's drum!
Praise and lament the chloroform that eases,
The spewing rock and acid tusk,
Eases an easy way and empties glasses.
Than such a coward poison sooner trust
A full vessel
Spilt not on Onan's mat,
And than the doctor's morsel
Longer if not so sweet.

July 9 '33

Forty Four

Too many times my same sick cry
Has rattled in a bag of words,
Too many times new notes I play
Have struck the same sick chords.
My thoughts may be a flock of birds
A shout can drive away,
A pack of cards a little breath blow down,
For though I utter all the day

My meaning in my little way,
You close your ears or call me clown.
Death and his sickle still alarm you,
Though very little can they harm you,
And god is still a deacon in the clouds;
Well, keep your fancies fat; time and again
I'll echo my old words.

July 9 '33

Forty Five

We have the fairy tales by heart,
No longer tremble at a bishop's hat,
And the thunder's first note;
We have these little things off pat,
Avoid church as a rot;
We scorn the juggernaut,
And the great wheels' rut;
Half of the old gang's shot,
Thank God, but the enemy stays put.

We know our Mother Goose and Eden,
No longer fear the walker in the garden,
And the fibs for children;
The old spells are undone.
But still ghosts madden,
A cupboard skeleton
Raises the hairs of lad and maiden.

If dead men walked they, too, would holler
At sight of death, the last two fisted killer
Stained a blood colour;
A panic's pallor
Would turn the dead yellow.

We have by heart the children's stories,
Have blown sky high the nursery of fairies;

Still a world of furies
Burns in many mirrors.

Death and evil are twin spectres.
What shall destruction count if these are fixtures?
Why blot the pictures
Of elves and satyrs
If these two gnomes remain unmoved by strictures?

We have the stories backwards,
Torn out magic from the hearts of cowards
By nape and gizzards;
There are two laggards,
Death and evil, too slow in heeding words.

Tear by the roots these twin growths in your gut;
Shall we learn fairy tales off pat,
Not benefit from that?
Burn out the lasting rot,
For death as little as the thunder's shot,
The holy hat.

July 14 '33

Forty Six

'Find meat on bones that soon have none
And drink in the two milked crags;
Eat till all's gone, drink to the dregs
Before the waxred breasts are hags
And the limbs are worn.
Disturb no winding sheets, my son,
But when the fodder's cold as stone
Then hang a ram rose over the rags.

Rebel against the binding moon
And the parliament of sky,
The kingcraft of the cunning sea,

171

Autocracy of night and day,
Dictatorship of sun;
Rebel against the flesh and bone,
The seed and blood, the jailing skin,
And the maggot no man can slay.'

'The thirst is quenched, the hunger gone,
And my heart is cracked across;
My face is haggard in the glass,
My lips are withered with a kiss,
My breasts are thin.
A lovely girl took me for man;
I laid her down, and told her sin,
And put beside her a ram rose.

The maggot that no man can kill
And the bird no bullet sting
Rebel against the reason's wrong
That penetrates the drum and lung
And cataracts the soul.
I cannot murder, like a fool,
Season and sunlight, grace and girl,
Nor can I smother the soul's waking.

The stars still minister the moon,
And the sky lays down the laws;
The sea speaks in a kingly voice;
Night and day are no enemies
But one companion.
"War on the spider and the wren!
War on the destiny of man!
Doom on the sun!"
Before death takes you, O take back this.'

July 15 '33

172

Forty Seven

Ears in the turrets hear
Hands grumble on the door,
Eyes in the gables see
The fingers at the locks.
Shall I unbolt or stay
Alone to the day I die,
Unseen by stranger-eyes,
In this white house?
Hands, hold you poison or grapes?

Beyond this island, bound
By a thin sea of flesh
And a bone coast,
The land lies out of sound,
And the hills out of mind.
No bird or flying fish
Disturbs this island's rest.

Ears in this island hear
The wind pass like a fire,
Eyes in this island see
Ships anchor off the bay.
Shall I run to the ships,
With the wind in my hair,
Or stay to the day I die,
And welcome no sailor?
Ships, hold you poison or grapes?

Hands grumble on the door,
Ships anchor off the bay,
Rain beats the sand and slates.
Shall I let in the stranger,
Shall I welcome the sailor,
Or stay to the day I die?

Hands of the stranger and holds of the ships,
Hold you poison or grapes?

July 17, '33

Forty Eight

(From A Play)

The Woman Speaks:
    No food suffices but the food of death;
    Sweet is the waxen blood, honey the falling flesh;
    There is no fountain springing from the earth
    Cool as the waxred fountains of the veins;
    No cradle's warmer than this perished breast,
    And hid behind the fortress of the ribs
    The heart lies ready for the raven's mouth,
    And lustreless within the ruined face
    The eyes remark the antics of the hawk.

    A sniper laid him low and strewed his brains;
    One would not think the greenness of this valley
    Could in a day be sick with so much blood;
    What were young limbs are faggots on the land,
    And young guts dry beneath the sickened sun.
    Let me not think, O God of carnage,
    Of ravens at the hero's meat and nerves
    Pecking and nestling all the time of night.

    The grass he covers is a pretty green;
    He has the still moon and the hundred stars;
    He learns the carrion pickers of the sky,
    And on his shoulders fall their world of wings,
    And on his ears hosannas of the grave.

    His narrow house is walled with blades of grass,
    Roofed with the sky and patterned with blond bones;
    The birds make him his cerements of plumes,
    Cerecloth of weed, and build an ordured bed.

    Since the first flesh of man was riven
    By scalpel lightning from the rifted sky,
    Man's marrow barbed, and breast ripped with a steel,

All that was loved and loved made the fowls' food,
Grief, like an open wound, has cried to heaven.

No food suffices but the food of death;
Death's appetite is sharpened by the bullet's thumb;
Yet he is dead, and still by woman's womb
Hungers for quickening, and my lonely lips
Hunger for him who dungs the valley fields.

There shall be no mute mourning over his acre,
Sorrow shall have no words, no willow wearing;
Rain shall defile and cover, wind bear away
The saddest dust in all this hollow world.

Old men whose blood is hindered in their veins,
Whom cancer crops, whose drinking rusts, these die;
These die who shovel the last home of man;
The sniper dies; the fingers from the sky
Strangle the little children in their beds;
One day my woman's body will be cold.

So I have come to know, but knowledge aches;
I know that age is snow upon the hair,
Wind carven lines around the drooping mouth;
And raven youth will feast but where he will.

Since the first womb spat forth a baby's corpse,
The mother's cry has fumed about the winds;
O tidal winds, cast up her cry for me;
That I may drown, let loose her flood of tears.

It was a haggard night the first flesh died,
And shafted hawks came snarling down the sky;
A mouse, it was, played with an ivory tooth,
And ravens fed confection to their young.

Palm of the earth, O sprinkle on my head
That dust you hold, O strew that little left;
Let what remains of that first miracle
Be sour in my hair. That I may learn

The mortal miracle, let that first dust
Tell me of him who feeds the raging birds.

July 33.

Fifty

Let the brain bear the hammering,
And heart the stabbing of the forks;
The devil hammers hell out of the ribs,
His playmates fork the skull.
The ears shall stand the clamouring,
Domdaniel shall not snip my sex;
I hear the little voices dropping jibes
As pigs' mouths drop their swill.
For all the devil's scissors I am male.
Let not the hands garotte,
The bullet wing, the bayonet gut;
The labyrinthine body must keep whole.

Be strong before my people fall,
The hair falls out, and tongues that foul
The dark dart at the ears of men.
The devil hammers hell out of the skull;
No bones shall break and no vein fail;
Beware the treaty and the gun.

August 33

Fifty One

The minute is a prisoner in the hour,
Lest brain keep watch will break its hours' cell
And play the truant in the den of days;
But arrow-eyed my senses shall not lose,

Nor sentinel my heart set free the frail
First vision that set fire to the air.

A minute wound that wonderment about,
When on the stivy wind a giant's voice
Told truth and rang the valley with its crying;
With falling wind down fell the giant's shout,
The meaning dropped and truth fled to the grass.
Deep in the valley's herbs I hear it dying.

Some see a living vision of the truth,
And some hear truth upon the wind, once only.
Forget, it dies, and lose, it's never found.
I shall remember losing until death,
Keep in my memory the minute lonely
Of truth that told the deaf and showed the blind.

August '33

Fifty Two

Shall gods be said to thump the clouds
When clouds are cursed by thunder,
Be said to weep when weather howls?
Shall rainbows be their tunics' colour?

When there is rain where are the gods?
Shall it be said they sprinkle water
From garden cans, or free the floods?

Shall it be said that, venuswise,
Some old god's dugs are pricked and pressed
When milky night is mother of the air?

Shall it be said that this moon's face
Is but the face reflected of some god
Admiring the acres of his brow?
Does gods' blood dye the sun?

177

It shall be said that gods are stone.
Shall a dropped stone thud on the ground,
Flung gravel chime? Let the stones speak
With tongues that talk all tongues.

The gods of stone our fathers worshipped
Are wood and brass if gods weep rain.
If gods thump thunder, then the clouds
Are gods and water, and the bark is brass.
All things are god if gods are thunder.

August.

Fifty Three

Matthias spat upon the lord
And gained an everlasting curse;
The Reverend Crap, a pious fraud,
Defiles his maker with a word
Dropped from those educated jaws.
Which is the most to be abhorred –
Jew's gob or gentile's praise?

The Reverend Crap, a holy pimp,
Reads the bible and loves children,
Loves to pat a choirboy's rump,
And, following the band of hope,
To stroke the girls behind the organ.
Who shall be cursed – the virgin Crap
Or the poxy whoreman?

August 16.

August 1933 Notebook

On the first page of this notebook, in addition to the announcement 'This Book Started 23rd August 1933', Thomas wrote an epigraph:

> To others caught
> Between black and white.

Thus, the parameters of the *August 1933 Notebook* can be thought of as the polarities that the young poet felt himself caught in, the forces of light and darkness, life and death, 'the green fuse' and 'the crooked worm'. There is little sense of development here, but rather the celebration and reiteration of process itself: 'O see the poles of promise.' And we are made to see process entirely through imagery, intensely physical imagery, mainly anatomical – no ideas, as it were, but in skulls. Thomas was very influenced by John Donne's *Devotions*, where Donne sees 'man as earth of the earth, his body earth, his hair a wild shrub growing out of the land' – so he told Pamela Hansford Johnson (who had written a fan letter immediately Thomas appeared in the *Sunday Referee* Poets' Corner in September 1933), continuing: 'The description of a thought or action – however abstruse it may be – can be beaten home by bringing it on to a physical level. Every idea, intuitive or intellectual, can be imaged and translated in terms of the body, its flesh, skin, blood, sinews, veins, glands, organs, cells, or senses' (*Letters* p. 39). While we have to admit, with Thomas himself

179

in another letter (sending five of these notebook poems to Trevor Hughes in January 1934), that, taken in large quantities, these poems seem 'unpretty things ... the perhaps wearisome succession of blood and bones, the neverending similes of the streams in the veins and the lights in the eyes' (*Letters* p. 90), we must also acknowledge that the power of Thomas's first volume, *18 Poems* (December 1934), was due to a consistency of energetic diction developed in the *August 1933 Notebook*. Indeed, thirteen of the eighteen poems of that volume came directly from this last notebook. It is here, then, that one can sense the increasing pressure of the poems themselves, pushing one against the next, forcing *18 Poems* into existence, and Thomas into immediate celebrity as the most original poet of his generation.

One

To A.E.T.

The hand that signed the paper felled a city;
Five sovereign fingers taxed the breath,
Doubled the globe of dead and halved a country;
These five kings did a king to death.

The mighty hand leads to a sloping shoulder,
The finger joints are cramped with chalk;
A goose's quill has put an end to murder
That put an end to talk.

The hand that signed the treaty bred a fever,
And famine grew, and locusts came;
Great is the hand that holds dominion over
Man by a scribbled name.

The fingers count the dead but do not soften
The crusted wounds nor pat the brow;
The hand rules pity as a hand rules heaven;
Hands have no tears to flow.

These five blind kings have quills for sceptres;
Each has a parchment for his shield,
Debates with vizier words what time he shatters
The four walls of the world.

August 17 '33.

Two

To T.H.

Let for one moment a faith statement
Rule the blank sheet of sleep,
The virgin lines be mated with a circle.
A circle spins. Let each revolving spoke
Turn and churn nightseed till it curdle.

181

Let for one moment a faith statement
Strip the dreams' livery,
And gods be changed as often as the shift.
God is the same though he be praised as many,
Remains though gods be felled till none are left.

Let for one moment a faith statement
See the first living light,
And your maieutic slumber drag it forth.
The child tells, when the trembling cord is cut,
God shall be gods and many deaths be death.

August 20, 33.
Rayner's Lane.

Three

You are the ruler of this realm of flesh,
And this hill of bone and hair
Moves to the Mahomet of your hand.
But all this land gives off a charnel stench,
The wind smacks of the poor
Dumb dead the crannies house and hide.

You rule the thudding heart that bites the side;
The heart steps to death's finger,
The brain acts to the legal dead.
Why should I think on death when you are ruler?

You are my flesh's ruler whom I treason,
Housing death in your kingdom,
Paying heed to the thirsty voice.
Condemn me to an everlasting facing
Of the dead eyes of children
And their rivers of blood turned to ice.

August 22 '33.

182

Four

That the sum sanity might add to nought
And matrons ring the harebells on their lips,
Girls woo the weather through the Sabbath night
And rock twin floods upon their starry laps,
I would enforce the black apparelled flocks,
And raise a hallelujah to the Lamb,
Trace on my breast a covert crucifix;
I would be woven at the Sabbath loom.

I would be woven a religious shape;
That earth might reel upon its block of reason
I would resound the heavens with my homage,
I would make genuflexion with the sheep
That men might holla, when the dawn has risen,
At day burnt bright by one fanatic image.

August 24 '33.

Five

Grief, thief of time, crawls off
With wasted years and half
The loaded span of days.
Marauding pain steals off
With half the load of faith
That weighed thee to thy knees.

The old forget their cries,
Lean times on evil seas,
And times the wind blew rough,
Remember the sea-boys
Riding sea-bear and horse
Over the salty path.

The old forget the grief,
And the hack of the cough,

And the friends fed to crows,
Remember the sea-youth,
And plucking wild radish,
And seed that was promise.

Grief is the price of peace,
And age forgets the cries,
The thief of time steals death.
Forget the prince's price,
Remember all thy days
Thy thieven load of faith.

August 26, '33.

Six

Shiloh's seed shall not be sown
In the garden of the womb
By a salty dropsy sipping,
No Redeemer shall be born
In the belly of a lamb
Dumbly and divinely leaping
Over the godbearing green.

From the meadow where lambs frolic
Rises every blade the Lamb,
From the heavens falls a dove.
Now is sun and summer phallic,
Promise is its fiery limb,
And a baby god its thief,
Thieving bone and flesh's tunic.

Through the floodgates of the sky
Grains of seed shall be dropped loose,
Manna for the hungry globe,
Quickening for the land and sea.
Settling in a virgin sluice,
It shall hammer at the rib,
Wall of wood or side of hay.

Prince's seed shall find a harbour,
A hundred wombs shall say him nay,
A hundred virgins hide him.
May a humble village labour,
And a continent deny?
A hemisphere may scold him,
And a green plot be his bearer.

The wren may warm him in her nest,
A water catch and cover
One falling grain, it knows not why,
And diggers find him in the dust.
With falling night a saviour,
A saviour with the break of day
Falls and is found, falls and is lost.

If veins are flowing with their juice,
It matters not if wood or brass,
Or man or woman, chances
Upon a fallen grain.
If veins are dry, the fortune changes;
If flesh hangs ragged on the bone,
The miracle shall change its face.

Life must stir before the seed,
And before the twilight sleep.
Brass must shudder, water swirl,
Sap must rustle in the wood.
And the dove shall fill its crop
Before the brazen Dove is whole
And the wooden Lamb is God.

Shiloh's seed shall not be sown
In the pastures of the worm;
Not in the fanatic womb
Shall the jelly mix and form
That shall be the three in One,
God and Ghost, Anointed Son.

August 29 33.

Seven

Before I knocked and flesh let enter,
With liquid hands tapped on the womb,
I who was shapeless as the water
That shaped the Jordan near my home,
Was the brother to Mnetha's daughter
And sister to the fathering worm.

I who was deaf to spring and summer,
Who knew not sun or moon by name,
Felt thud beneath my flesh's armour
As yet was in a molten form,
The leaden stars, the rainy hammer
Swung by my father from his dome.

I knew the message of the winter,
The darted hail, the childish snow,
And the wind was my sister suitor;
Wind in me leaped, the hellborn dew;
My veins flowed with the valley weather;
Ungotten I knew night and day.

As yet ungotten, I did suffer;
The rack of dreams my lily bones
Did twist into a living cipher,
And flesh was snipped to cross the lines
Of gallow crosses on the liver
And brambles in the wringing brains.

My milk was curdled by the thunder;
The lightning forked into the jaw,
The lilac gums, that kissed me murder;
Deep in my bowels jumped the fire,
The false lips cursed me like an adder
Who bares his sting to wound the air.

My throat knew thirst before the structure
Of skin and vein around the well

Where words and water make a mixture
Unfailing till the blood runs foul;
My heart knew love, my belly hunger,
I smelt the maggot in my stool.

And time cast forth my mortal creature
To drift or drown upon the seas
Acquainted with the salt adventure
Of tides that never touch the shores.
I who was rich was made the richer
By sipping at the vine of days.

I, born of flesh and ghost, was neither
A ghost or man, but mortal ghost.
And I was struck down by death's feather.
I was mortal to the last
Long breath that carried to my father
The message of his dying Christ.

A virgin was my sad-faced dam,
My sire was of wind and water.
Get thee behind me, my blood's tempter,
I cried out when the blood was dumb.

You who bow down at cross and altar,
Remember me and pity him
Who took my flesh and bone for armour,
And double-crossed his mother's womb.

September 6

Eight

We see rise the secret wind behind the brain,
The sphinx of light sit on the eyes,
The code of stars translate in heaven.
A secret night descends between
The skull, the cells, the cabinned ears
Holding for ever the dead moon.

187

A shout went up to heaven like a rocket,
Woe from the rabble of the blind
Adorners of the city's forehead,
Gilders of streets, the rabble hand
Saluting the busy brotherhood
Of rod and wheel that wake the dead.

A city godhead, turbine moved, steel sculptured,
Glitters in the electric streets;
A city saviour, in the orchard
Of lamp-posts and high-volted fruits,
Speaks a steel gospel to the wretched
Wheel-winders and fixers of bolts.

We hear rise the secret wind behind the brain,
The secret voice cry in our ears,
The city gospel shout to heaven.
Over the electric godhead grows
One God, more mighty than the sun.
The cities have not robbed our eyes.

September 8.

Nine

Take the needles and the knives,
Put an iron at the eyes,
Let a maggot at the ear
Toil away till music dies.

Let me in the devil's groves
Cut my fingers on a rose,
Let the maggot of despair
Drain the spring where promise goes.

Take the scissors and the pan,
Let the tiny armies lap,
And the heralds of decay,
At the labyrinthine pap.

188

Choke the bladder with a stone,
Fill the veins the fevers broke,
All the beggar faiths deny
And the feeble house of hope.

And a child might be my slayer,
And a mother in her labour
Murder with a cry of pain;
Half a smile might be her sabre.

Let it be a sword of fire,
Lightning or the darting viper,
Thunder's rod or man's machine;
God and I will pay the sniper.

Flesh is suffered, is laid low,
Mixes, ripens, in the loam;
Spirit suffers but is still
In its labyrinthine home.

In the wilderness they go,
Flesh and spirit, babe and dam,
Walking in the evening's cool
With the leper and the lamb.

In the darkness dam and babe
Tremble at the starry stain,
And the ruin of the sky;
Darkness is the dam of pain.

Take the scissors to this globe,
Firmament of flesh and bone
Lawed and ordered from on high
By a godhead of my own.

Mother root that shot me forth,
Like a green tree through the sward,
Mothers me until I die,
And my father was the lord.

When I yield the tree to death,
In the country of the dead
Dam and sire, living, lo,
Will be breathing by my bed.

Take the needles to this tree
Bowing on its mossy knees,
Stitch the stem on to the leaf,
Let the sap leak in the breeze.

Thread and torture all the day;
You but wound the lord of days;
Slay me, slay the god of love;
God is slain in many ways.

Question: Shall the root be true
And the green tree trust the root?
Answer: Shall a mother lie
In the face of seed and fruit?

Question: When shall root-dam die?
Answer: When her babe denies her.
Question: When shall root-dam grow?
Answer: When the green leaves prize her.

September 12.

Ten

To B.C.

Not forever shall the lord of the red hail
Hold in his velvet hand the can of blood;
He shall be wise and let his brimstone spill,
Free from their burning nests the arrows' brood.
And sweet shall fall contagion from his side,
And loud his anger stamp upon the hill.

As fire falls, two hemispheres divide,
The fields yet undivined behind the skull
Are made divine by every lightning rod,
And perish as the level lands of steel.
Both mind and matter at the golden word
Shall fall away, and leave one singing shell.

A hole in space shall keep the shape of thought,
The lines of earth, the curving of the heart,
And from this darkness spin the golden soul.
Intangible my world shall come to nought,
The solid world shall wither in the heat,
How soon, how soon, o lord of the red hail!

September 15. '33
Llangain Carms.

Eleven

Before we mothernaked fall
Upon the land of gold or oil
Between the raid and the response
    Of flesh and bones
Our claim is staked for once and all
Near to the quarry or the well
Before the promises fulfill
    And joys are pains.

Then take the gusher or the field
Where all the hidden stones are gold
We have no choice our choice was made
    Before our blood
And I will build my liquid world
And you, before the breath is cold
And doom is turned and veins are spilled,
    Your solid land.

Choose the field of brick and bone
Or the dark well of the brain
Take one away let one remain.
    All is foreknown.

September 16. 33.
Llangain

Twelve

The sun burns the morning, a bush in the brain;
Moon walks the river and raises the dead;
Here in my wilderness wanders the blood;
And the sweat on the brow makes a sign,
And the wailing heart's nailed to the side.

Here is a universe bred in the bone,
Here is a saviour who sings like a bird,
Here the night shelters and here the stars shine,
Here a mild baby speaks his first word
In the Bethlehem under the skin.

Under the ribs sail the moon and the sun;
A cross is tatooed on the breast of the child,
And sewn on his skull a scarlet thorn;
For the price of Christ is paid in pain,
And a labouring mother pays twofold.

September 16.
Llangain

Thirteen

My hero bares his nerves along my wrist
That rules from wrist to shoulder
Unpacks the head that like a sleepy ghost
Leans on my mortal ruler
The proud spine spurning turn and twist.

And these poor nerves so wired to the skull
Ache on the lovelorn paper
I hug to love with my unruly scrawl
That utters all love-hunger
And tells the page the empty ill.

My hero bares my side and sees his heart
Tread like a naked Venus
The beach of flesh and wind her bloodred plait;
Stripping my loin of promise
He promises a secret heat.

He holds the wire from this box of nerves
Turning the mortal error
Of birth and death the two sad knaves of thieves
And the hunger's emperor;
He pulls the chain the cistern moves.

Jack my father let the knaves steal off
Their little swag, the gems of life and death,
The lightest bubbles that we breathe
Out of the living grave
And let my hero show his double strength
And all his laughter hidden up my sleeve.

September 17 '33.
Llangain

Fifteen

In the beginning was the three-pointed star,
One smile of light across the empty face;
One rib of flesh across the frame of air,
The substance spread that moulded the first sun;
And heaven was, a cloudy hole, and hell
A burning stick across the bum of space.

In the beginning was the dim signature
Spelt with the three syllables of light,

193

And after came the imprints of the water,
Stamp of the minted face upon the moon;
The blood that touched the brim of Joseph's grail
Touched the first sky and left a living clot.

In the beginning was the three-eyed prick,
The red eyed genitor of mind and matter,
Set on the stone of space, the ageing rock
As empty as a skeleton's ear;
And roots exploded in the powdered land,
And there were trees and there was water.

In the beginning was the word, the word
That was all words and one, the word of time,
The word of darkness and the spinning void;
The star translated into all-tongued light
The word of peace, of time, one word and all,
The three-eyed word spelling a single name.

In the beginning was a secret thought,
Before the word was lodged in the clouds' mouth
And the first star changed all the sounds to light;
In the beginning was the house of air
Ruled by the thought to be the word and hand,
The prayer and deed, the body and the breath.

September 18 '33
Llangain.

Sixteen

Love me, not as the dreamy nurses
My falling lungs, nor as the cypress
In his age the lass's clay.
Love me and lift your mask.

194

Love me, not as the girls of heaven
Their airy lovers, nor the mermaiden
Her salt lovers in the sea.
Love me and lift your mask.

Love me, not as the ruffling pigeon
The tops of trees, nor as the legion
Of the gulls the lip of waves.
Love me and lift your mask.

Love me, as loves the mole his darkness
And the timid deer the tigress:
Hate and fear be your twin loves.
Love me and lift your mask.

September 18. '33.

In Three Parts

Seventeen
(Part One)

For loss of blood I fell where stony hills
Had milk and honey flowing from their cracks,
And where the footed dew was on the pools
I knelt to drink the water dry as sticks.
Where was no water ran the honeyed milks,
And where was water was the drybacked sand.

I met the ghost of water on the paths,
And knelt before the ghostly man of milk;
Where was no honey were the humming wraiths
Descending on the flowers' cup and stalk.
Where was no water there the image rides,
And where was water was the stony hand.

For lack of faith I fell upon the desert
Where eagles tenanted the single palm;
Where was no god I heard his windy visit,

195

And saw the spider weave him on her loom.
And where god was his holy house was sculptured,
A monster lie upon the middened land.

I fell upon the ugly vales and wept;
The ravens crowed to spy my drooping eyes,
And with their crowing was my wet grief stopped,
A feather said a blessing from the trees;
And, pretty here, a malediction stirs,
Upon these slopes is burnt a killer's brand.

For lack of love I fell where love was not,
The plains by the still sea, and there love sat,
My child did knock within her happy heart.
And where love was sat fever on her throne,
My child did scream and burn within her womb
And where love lay was laid her hot-veined brat.

At last I came to a remembered cave,
There made my lodge, and sucked the fallen figs,
Where no thief walked leapt through my neighbour's grove,
My skin not waxen old upon my dugs.
Where no thief was there came the padded knave
To set his famined hands upon my fat.

The thief of light did sew upon my lids
His chequered shades, and at my open ear
The thief of sound poured down his fluids,
The thief of speech was busy at the jaw.
When all was peace there came these palming lads
To nick my senses but to leave the breath.

And all was dim, and stilly went the wind,
Under my granite roof I lay and healed,
And peace was with me as a pleasant sound.
When all was peace there came the thieving king,
Sat at my feet and told this summing song:
When all is lost is paid the sum of death.

September 25 33.

Eighteen
(Part Two)

Jack my father, let the knaves
Fill with a swag of bubbles their sad sacks,
No fingers press their fingers on the wax
Red as the axe, blue as a hanging man.

Jack my father, let the thieves
Share their fool spoil with their sad brood of sneaks,
No silver whistles chase them down the weeks'
Daybouldered peaks into the iron van.

Let them escape, the living graves
Be bared of loveliness and shorn of sex,
Let sense be plundered and the dryboned wrecks
Of words perplex the sad tides of the brain.

Let them run off with laden sleeves,
These stolen bubbles have the bites of snakes,
These sacked wines raise a thirst no liquor slakes,
No victual breaks this hunger son of pain.

Lust and love both be your loves,
Wean the well-loved on one symmetric breast,
Please the one-minded hand, and suck to rest
The body pressed upon one flesh and bone.

One dies all die, all live one lives,
And slopes and vales are blessed as they are cursed;
Both sweet and bitter were the last and first
Truths to be nursed with their same mother's groan.

Where is no god there man believes,
And where god is his homage turns to dust;

God who is all tells in his desert gust
That one man must be all and all be one.

When the knave of death arrives,
Yield the lost flesh to him and give your ghost;
All shall remain, and on the cloudy coast
Walk the blithe host
Of god and ghost with you, their newborn son.

September 26. '33.

Nineteen
(Part Three)

The girl, unlacing, trusts her breast,
Doubts not its tint nor how it leans;
Faith in her flesh maintains its shape
From toe to head.
Their maiden cloths the stars unslip,
And from her shift the worn moon turns
One bosom to her lover's bed
Red in the east.

Should the girl doubt, a sallow ring
Would rim her eyes and sphere her breast;
And should the stars blush as they strip,
Ashamed of light,
Their manypointed light would drop;
If the moon doubts, her dew is dust;
If day lacks faith, it turns to night,
And light is done.

It shall happen that time's venom
Darts to your cheek and leaves its scars;
Burning like age upon your mouth,
The old-veined wind
Shall bear away the kiss of youth;
And it shall happen that the stars,
Lorn of their naked welcome,
Shoot as they fade.

Trust, in the first, the desert hills,
And milk will move along their udders;
Let the hilly milk sit sweet
Upon the tongue,
And honey quiet every gut;
Trust the lips the honey colours:
Lips shall be smiling, always young,
Though the flesh falls.

The girl, unlacing, trusts her breast:
Forever shall the breast give milk;
The naked star stands unashamed:
It shall forever.
You who believe the stony hand,
And, groaning, trust the needles' stroke,
Shall be star-fathered on the air
And Jack of Christ.

September 29 '33.

Twenty

Through these lashed rings set deep inside their hollows
I eye the ring of earth, the airy circle,
My Maker's flesh that garments my clayfellows.
And through these trembling rings set in their valley
Whereon the hooded hair casts down its girdle,
A holy voice acquaints me with His glory.

Through these two rounded lips I pray to heaven,
Unending sea around my measured isle
The water spirit moves as it is bidden;
And, with not one fear-beggared syllable,
Praise God who springs and fills the tidal well;
Through this heart's pit I know His miracle.

And through these eyes God marks myself revolving,
And from these tongue-plucked senses draws his tune;
Inside this mouth I feel his message moving
Acquainting me with my divinity;
And through these ears he harks my fire burn
His awkward heart into some symmetry.

September 30. '33.

Twenty One

Ape and ass both spit me forth,
I am spawn of leech and frog;
Crawling from the serpent's egg
I am born to breed and breathe.

Couch I in the weasel's bag,
Suck I at the monkey's thumb;
From the shell I show a leg
Thin as a crow's womb.

Got together sow and pig,
I was franked in the sow's side;
I am son of fish and bird,
Daughter of the ferret's hug.

Twenty Two

The eye of sleep turned on me like a moon,
Let fall the tear of time; the hand of sleep
Let fall the snail of time and wound his horn.
So, featherheeled, I journeyed through a dream,
And had the lip of darkness on my lip.

I fled the earth, and, naked, climbed the weather,
Reaching a second ground, far from the stars;
And there we wept, I and a ghostly other,

My mother-eyed, upon the tops of trees;
I fled the ground, as lightly as a feather.

I climbed a cloud, and poised above the earth,
Ghost at my arm, and dawn about my head;
And soon the mouth of darkness at my mouth
Kissed and was answered as the kiss of death;
For dark I spoke and the black ghost replied.

'My father's globe knocks on its nave, and sings'.
'This that we tread was, too, thy father's land'.
'But this we tread bears the angelic gangs,
Sweet are their fathered faces in their wings'.
'These are but dreaming men: breathe, and they fade'.

I breathed aloud, and with the fading men
Faded my elbow-ghost, the mother-eyed.
And on the airy steps I climbed again,
Over the prick of earth, towards a plane
Set near the stars and by the weak moon-side.

There all the matter of the living air
Raised its harmonious voice; the pulse of God
Hammered within the circling roads of fire;
There was the song of God the singing core
Under the gravecloths of the cloudy dead.

Around me shone the faces of the spheres,
And hung the comets' hair, the meteor ropes
Whereby I swarmed up to the starry spires.
Beneath me leapt the salamandrine furies
Out of the half moon where a mad man sleeps.

And stripped I stood upon a columned cloud,
Fear at my heart of all the laws of heaven
And the mysterious order of the Lord.
And, like a bloodred-ribbon where I stood
There grew the hours' ladder to the sun.

Oct 5 '33.

201

Twenty Three

To E.P.

The force that through the green fuse drives the flower
Drives my green age, that blasts the roots of trees
Is my destroyer.
And I am dumb to tell the crookèd rose
My youth is bent by the same wintry fever.

The force that drives the water through the rocks
Drives my red blood; that dries the mouthing streams
Turns mine to wax.
And I am dumb to mouth unto my veins
How at the mountain spring the same mouth sucks.

The hand that whirls the water in the pool
Stirs the quicksand; that ropes the blowing wind
Hauls my shroud sail.
And I am dumb to tell the hanging man
How of my clay is made the hangman's lime.

The lips of time leech to the fountain head;
Love drips and gathers, but the fallen blood
Shall make her well;
And I am dumb to tell the timeless sun
How time has ticked a heaven round the stars.

And I am dumb to tell the lover's tomb
How at my sheet goes the same crookèd worm.

October 12. '33

Twenty Four

From love's first fever to her plague, from the soft second
And to the hollow minute of the womb,
From the unfolding to the scissored caul,
The time for breast and the green apron age
When no mouth stirred about the hanging famine,

All world was one, one windy nothing,
My world was christened in a stream of milk.
And earth and sky were as one airy hill,
The sun and moon shed one white light.

From the first print of the unshodden foot, the lifting
Hand, the hatching of the hair,
And to the miracle of the first rounded word,
From the first secret of the heart, the warning ghost,
And to the first dumb wonder at the flesh,
The sun was red, the moon was gray,
The earth and sky were as two mountains meeting.

The body prospered, teeth in the marrowed gums,
The growing bones, the rumour of manseed
Within the hallowed gland, blood blessed the heart,
And the four winds, that had long blown as one,
Shone in my ears the light of sound,
Called in my eyes the sound of light,
And where one globe had spun a host did circle
The nave of heaven, each with his note.
And yellow was the multiplying sand,
Each golden grain spat life into its fellow,
Green was the singing house.

The plum my mother picked matured slowly,
The boy she dropped from darkness at her side
Into the sided lap of light, grew strong,
Was muscled, matted, wise to the crying thigh
And to the voice that, like a voice of hunger,
Itched in the noise of wind and sun.

(Incomplete)

October 14 '33

Twenty Five

The almanac of time hangs in the brain;
The seasons numbered by the inward sun,
The winter years, move in the pit of man;
His graph is measured as the page of pain
Shifts to the redwombed pen.

The calendar of age hangs in the heart,
A lover's thought tears down the dated sheet,
The inch of time's protracted to a foot
By youth and age, the mortal state and thought
Ageing both day and night.

The word of time lies on the chaptered bone,
The seed of time is sheltered in the loin;
The grains of life must seethe beneath the sun,
The syllables be said and said again:
Time shall belong to man.

October 16. 33

Twenty Six
(Continuation of Twenty Four)

And from the first declension of the flesh
I learnt man's tongue, to twist the shapes of thoughts
Into the stony idiom of the brain,
To shade and knit anew the patch of words
Left by the dead who, in their moonless acre,
Need no word's warmth.
The root of tongues ends in a spentout cancer,
That but a name, where maggots have their X.

I learnt the verbs of will, and had my secret;
The code of night tapped on my tongue;

What had been one was many sounding minded.

One womb, one mind, spewed out the matter,
One breast gave suck, the fever's issue;
From the divorcing sky I learnt the double,
The two-framed globe that spun into a score;
A million minds gave suck to such a bud
As forked my eye.
Youth did condense: the tears of spring
Dissolved in summer and the hundred seasons;
One sun, one manna, warmed and fed.

Now that drugged youth is waking from its stupor,
The nervous hand rehearsing on the thigh
Acts with a woman, one sum remains in cipher:
Five senses and the frozen brain
Are one with wind, and itching in the sun.
Stone is my mate? who shall brass be?
What seed to me?
The soldered world debates.

How are they seeded, all that move,
With all that move not to the eye?
What seed, what seed to me?

October 17 '33

Twenty Seven

All that I owe the fellows of the grave
And all the dead bequeath from pale estates
Lies in the fortuned bone, the flask of blood,
Like senna stirs along the ravaged roots.
O all I owe is all the flesh inherits,
My fathers' loves that pull upon my nerves,
My sisters' tears that sing upon my head,
My brothers' blood that salts my open wounds.

Heir to the scalding veins that hold love's drop,
My fallen filled, that had the hint of death,
Heir to the telling senses that alone
Acquaint the flesh with a remembered itch,
I round this heritage as rounds the sun
His winy sky, and, as the candle's moon,
Cast light upon my weather. I am heir
To women who have twisted their last smile,
To children who were suckled on a plague,
To young adorers dying on a kiss.
All such disease I doctor in my blood,
And all such love's a shrub sown in the breath.

Then look, my eyes, upon this bonebound fortune
And browse upon the postures of the dead;
All night and day I eye the ragged globe
Through periscopes rightsighted from the grave;
All night and day I wander in these same
Wax clothes that wax upon the ageing ribs;
All night my fortune slumbers in its sheet.
Then look, my heart, upon the scarlet trove,
And look, my grain, upon the falling wheat;
All night my fortune slumbers in its sheet.

Twenty Eight

Here lie the beasts of man and here I feast,
The dead man said,
And silently I milk the devil's breast.
Here spring the silent venoms of his blood,
Here clings the meat to sever from his side.
Hell's in the dust.

Here lies the beast of man and here his angels,
The dead man said,
And silently I milk the buried flowers.
Here drips a silent honey in my shroud,
Here slips the ghost who made of my pale bed
The heaven's house.

October 25 33.
Llangain.

Twenty Nine

When once the twilight locks no longer
Locked in the long worm of my finger
Nor damned the sea that sped about my fist,
The mouth of time sucked, like a sponge,
The milky acid on each hinge,
And swallowed dry the waters of the breast.

When the galactic sea was sucked
And all the dry sea bed unlocked,
Rose the dry ghost of night to suck the day;
No hyleg but the Sleeper's star
Shone on this globe of bone and hair,
No star but sleep's was nodding in the sky.

Some dead upon a slab of wind
Where middle darkness spins around
Undid their lungs and leaked their midnight seed;

207

Along the wind the dead men drove
The redhaired cancer at their stuff,
And drove the midge that fluttered in their blood.

The horrors took the shapes of thoughts,
The wings of flies, the tails of rats,
And, cancervoiced, did crow upon my heap;
The midge that put a fever in
The bag of blood that swelled a vein
Hopped in my eyes and drew the straws of sleep.

The issue armoured, of the grave
Of violet fungus still alive
And winking eyes that catch the eye of death;
The seed of dreams that showed a bud
Through dust and sleep nods in my side;
Sleep is the winding lover in my cloth.

Sleep navigates the tides of time;
The dry Sargasso of the tomb
Gives up its dead to the divining hours;
And sleep drags up the kicking heart,
The driving brains, the brain of night
That day put down as age knocks down the flowers.

Crow on my heap, O living deaths;
There is no horror death bequeaths
I cannot number on this sleepy hand;
The golden emerods of the sun,
The dung that cometh out of man,
Spread in my sleep that makes the stars go round.

A sweet shrub rises from the wrecks
And sprouts between the coffin's crack;
The cypress dead are singing in the yard;
My sleep is scented by the shrub
That scents the dead man in his robe,
My sins fly through the window like a bird.

There is no sweetness in the dead
I feel not in my sleeping blood;
Then sleep and dream, sleeps dreams and dies;
When once the twilight locks no longer
Locked in the long worm of my finger
I did unlock the Sleeper's eyes.

November 11. 33.

Thirty

Light breaks where no sun shines;
Where no sea runs, the waters of the heart
Push in their tides;
And, broken ghosts with glow-worms in their heads,
The things of light
File through the flesh where no flesh decks the bones.

A candle in the thighs
Warms youth and seed, and burns the seeds of age;
Where no seed stirs
The fruit of man unwrinkles in the stars,
Bright as a fig;
Where no wax is the candle shows its hairs.

Dawn breaks behind the eyes;
From pole of skull and toe the windy blood
Slides like a sea;
Nor fenced, nor staked, the gushers of the sky
Spout to the rod
Divining in a smile the oil of tears.

Night in the sockets rounds,
Like some pitch moon, the limit of the globes;
Day lights the bone;
Where no cold is the skinning gales unpin
The winter's robes;
The film of spring is hanging from the lids.

Light breaks on secret lots,
On tips of thought, where thoughts smell in the rain;
When logics die
The secret of the soil grows through the eye,
And blood jumps in the sun;
Above the waste allotments the dawn halts.

November 20 33.

Thirty One

I fellowed sleep who kissed between the brains;
Her spinning kiss through my lean sheets
Stopped in the bones.
I fathered dreams as races from the loins
And sleep, pit-wombed, who kissed the pits.

Sleep shifts along the latches of the night;
The shifting night inched in as she
Drew back the bolt;
My fellow sleep who kissed me in the heart
With her salt hairs unlocked the sky.

I fellowed sleep who drained me with a kiss;
Where went but one grave-gabbing shade
Now go the stars;
Now stirs a ruined moon about my bed;
And worlds hang on the trees.

November 27th 33.

Thirty Two

See, says the lime, my wicked milks
I put round ribs that packed their heart,
And elbowed veins that, nudging blood,
Roused it to fire;

Once in this clay fenced by the sticks
That starry fence the clay of light
The howling spirit shaped a god
Of death's undoer.

On these blue lips, the lime remarks,
The wind of kisses sealed a pact
That leaping veins threw to the wind
And brains turned sour;
The blood got up as red as wax
As kisses froze the waxing thought,
The spirit racked its muscles and
The loins cried murder.

The strings of fire choked his sex
And tied an iris in his throat
To burst into a hanging land
Where flesh's fever
Itched on the hangman's silks;
The brains of death undid the knot
Before the blood and flame were twined
In love's last collar.

See, says the lime, around these wrecks
Of growing bones the muscles slid;
I chalked upon the breastbone's slate
And ran a river
Up through the fingers' cracks;
The milk of death, I filled the hand
That drove my stuff through skin and gut;
Death's death's undoer.

December 13 '33

211

Thirty Three

This bread I break was once the oat,
This wine upon a foreign tree
Plunged in its fruit;
Man in the day or wind at night
Laid the crops low, broke the grape's joy.

Once in this wine the summer blood
Knocked in the flesh that decked the vine,
Once in this bread
The oat was merry in the wind;
Man broke the sun, pulled the wind down.

This flesh you break, this blood you let
Make desolation in the vein,
Were oat and grape,
Born of the same sweet soil and sap.
My wine you drink, my bread you break.

Dec: 24 '33

Thirty Four

Your pain shall be a music in your string
And fill the mouths of heaven with your tongue
Your pain shall be
O my unborn
A vein of mine
Made fast by me.

Your string shall stretch a gully twixt the thumbs
Whose flaming blood shall rub it at the rims
Your pain shall be
O my unsown
A ragged vein
Twixt you and me.

Your pain shall be a meaning in your lips
As milk shall be a music in the paps
Your pain shall be
O my unknown
A stream of mine
Not milked by me.

Your pain shall not unmilk you of the food
That drops to make a music in your blood
Your pain shall be
O my undone
Flesh blood and bone
Surrounding me.

January 12. '34.

Thirty Five

A process in the weather of the heart
Turns damp to dry; the golden shot
Storms in the freezing grave.
A weather in the quarter of the veins
Turns night to day; blood in their suns
Lights up the living worm.

A process in the eye forewarns
The bones of blindness; and the womb
Drives in a death as life leaks out.

A darkness in the weather of the eye
Is half its light; the fathomed sea
Breaks on unangled land.
The seed that makes a forest of the loin
Forks half its fruit; and half drops down,
Slow in a sleeping wind.

A weather in the flesh and bone
Is damp and dry; the quick and dead

213

Move like two ghosts before the eye.

A process in the weather of the world
Turns ghost to ghost; each mothered child
Sits in their double shade.
A process blows the moon into the sun,
Pulls down the shabby curtains of the skin;
And the heart gives up its dead.

February 2. '34

Thirty Six

Foster the light, nor veil the bushy sun,
Nor sister moons that go not in the bone,
But strip and bless the marrow in the spheres;
Master the night, nor spite thy starry spine,
Nor muster worlds that spin not through the skin,
But know the clays that burrow round the stars.

Murmur of spring, nor crush the roaring eggs,
Nor hammer back the season in the figs,
But wind the summer-bearer in thy get;
Farmer the wilds, nor fill the corny bogs,
Nor harm a weed that wars not in thy legs,
But set and grow a meadow in thy heart.

And father all, nor fail with barren winds;
The weather moves like acid in thy glands;
The ass shall find a thistle in thy seed.
O gather all, nor leave the seas and sands
To cut and smother in a tide of wounds
One inch of flesh that glories in its blood.

But move unmarrowed in thy ragged shifts,
O sea and sky, nor sorrow as this flesh
Goes from another with a nitric smile;

Nor as my bones are bridled on her shafts,
Or when my locks are shooting in the turf,
Shalt thou fetch down the comets with a howl.

God gave the clouds their colours and their shapes;
He gave me clay, and dyed the crowded sea
With the green wings of fish and fairy men;
Set thou thy clouds and daylights on my lips,
Give me thy tempers and thy tides as I
Have given flesh unto the sea and moon.

February 23. '34.

Thirty Seven

I

The shades of girls all flavoured from their shrouds,
The bones of men, the broken in their beds,
Even the dancing ash,
When sunlight goes go dainty in the yards;
And even we, ascending through the lids,
Dance in our drowsy flesh.

The skeletons return when cocks go mad,
And dust and girl blow backward to their trash,
Night of the flesh is shaken of its blood,
Night of the brain stripped of its burning bush.

Our eunuch dreams, all seedless in the light,
Of light and love, the tempers of the heart,
Whack their boys' limbs,
And, winding-footed in their shawl and sheet,
Groom the dark brides, and widows of the night
Fold in their arms.

The brides return, freed from the starry knot,
The midnight pulleys that unhoused the tomb;

No children break, all flavoured into light
When love, awoken, hungers in her womb.

II

In this our age the gunman and his moll,
Two one-dimensioned ghosts, love on a reel,
Strange to my moony eye,
And speak their midnight nothings as they swell;
When cameras shut they hurry to their holes
Down in the yard of day.

They dance between their arclamps and my skull,
Impose their shots, throwing the nights away;
I watch the show of shadows kiss or kill,
Flavoured of celluloid give love the lie.

III

Which is the world? Of my two sleepings, which
Shall fall awake when cures and their itch
Raise up this red-eyed earth?
Pack off the shapes of daylight and their starch,
The sunny gentlemen, the Welshing rich,
Or drive the night-geared forth.

The photograph is married to the eye,
Grafts on its bride one-sided skins of truth;
The dream has sucked the sleeper of his faith
That shrouded men might marrow as they fly.

(continued)

This is the world: the lying likeness of
Our strips of stuff that tatter as we move
Loving and being loth;
The dream that kicks the buried from their sack

And lets their trash be honoured as the quick.
This is the world. Have faith.

For we shall be a shouter like the cock,
Blowing the old dead back; our shots shall smack
The image from the plates.
And we shall be fit fellows for a life,
And who remain shall flower as they love,
Praise to our faring hearts.

March '34.

Thirty Eight

Where once the waters of your face
Spun to my screws, your dry ghost blows,
The dead turns up its eye;
Where once the mermen through your ice
Pushed up their hair, the dry wind steers
Through salt and root and roe.

Where once your green knots sank their splice
Into the tided cord, there goes
The green unraveller,
His scissors oiled, his knife hung loose
To cut the channels at their course
And lay the salt fruits low.

Invisible, your clocking tides
Break on the love-beds of the weeds;
The weed of love's left dry;
There round about your stones the shades
Of children go who from their voids
Cry to the dolphined sea.

Dry as a tomb, your coloured lids
Shall not be latched while magic glides
Sage on the earth and sky;
There shall be corals in your beds,

217

There shall be serpents in your tides,
Till all our sea-faiths die.

March 18. '34.

Thirty Nine

I

I see the boys of summer in their ruin
Lay the gold tithings barren,
Setting no store by harvest freeze the soils;
There in their heat the winter floods
Of frozen loves they fetch their girls,
And drown the cargoed apples in their tides.

These boys of light are curdlers in their folly,
Sour the boiling honey,
The jacks of frost they finger in the hives;
There in the sun the frigid threads
Of doubt and dark they feed their nerves,
The signal moon is zero in their voids.

I see the summer children in their mothers
Split up the brawned womb's weathers,
Divide the night and day with fairy thumbs;
There in the deep with quartered shades
Of sun and moon they paint their dams
As sunlight paints the shelling of their heads.

I see that from these boys shall men of nothing
Stature by seedy shifting
Or lame the air with leaping from its heats;
There from their hearts the dogdayed pulse
Of love and light bursts in their throats.
Oh see the pulse of summer in the ice.

II

But seasons must be challenged or they totter
Into a chiming quarter
Where, punctual as death, we ring the stars;

There in his night the black-tongued bells
The sleepy man of winter pulls,
Nor blows back moon-and-midnight as she blows.

We are the dark deniers, let us summon
Death from a summer woman,
A muscling life from lovers in their cramp,
From the fair dead who flush the sea
The bright-eyed worm on Davy's lamp,
And from the planted womb the man of straw.

We summer boys in this four-winded spinning,
Green of the seaweeds' iron,
Hold up the noisy sea and drop her birds,
Pick the world's ball of wave and froth
To choke the deserts with her tides,
And comb the county gardens for a wreath.

In spring we cross our foreheads with the holly,
Heigh ho the blood and berry,
And nail the merry squires to the trees;
Here love's damp muscle dries and dies,
Here break a kiss in no love's quarry.
Oh see the poles of promise in the boys.

III

I see you boys of summer in your ruin.
Man in his maggot's barren.
And boys are full and foreign in the pouch.
I am the man your father was.
We are the sons of flint and pitch.
Oh see the poles are kissing as they cross!

April '34.

219

Forty

In the beginning was the three-pointed star,
One smile of light across the empty face;
One bough of bone across the rooting air,
The substance spread that marrowed the first sun;
And, burning ciphers on the round of space,
Heaven and hell mixed as they spun.

In the beginning was the pale signature,
Three-syllabled and starry as the smile;
And after came the imprints on the water,
Stamp of the minted face upon the moon;
The blood that touched the crosstree and the grail
Touched the first cloud and left a sign.

In the beginning was the mounting fire
That set alight the weathers from a spark,
A three-eyed, red-eyed spark blunt as a flower;
Life rose and spouted from the rolling seas,
Burst in the roots, pumped from the earth and rock
The secret oils that drive the grass.

In the beginning was the word, the word
That from the solid bases of the light
Abstracted all the letters of the void;
And from the cloudy bases of the breath
The word flowed up, translating to the heart
First characters of birth and death.

In the beginning was the secret brain;
The brain was celled and soldered in the thought
Before the pitch was forking to a sun;
Before the veins were shaking in their sieve,
And blood was scattered to the winds of light,
A secret heart rehearsed its love.

April. '34.

Forty One

If I was tickled by the rub of love,
A rooking girl who stole me for her side,
Broke through her straws, breaking my bandaged string,
If the red tickle as the cattle calve
Still set to scratch a laughter from my lung,
I would not fear the apple nor its flood
Nor the bad blood of spring.

Shall it be male or female? says the cells,
And drop the plum like fire from the flesh.
If I was tickled by the hatching hair,
The winging bone that sprouted in the heels,
The itch of man upon the baby's thigh,
I would not fear the gallows nor the axe
Nor the crossed sticks of war.

Shall it be male or female? say the fingers
Chalking the jakes with green things of the brain.
I would not fear the muscling-in of love
If I was tickled by the urchin hungers
Rehearsing heat upon a raw-edged nerve.
I would not fear the devil in the loin
Nor the outspoken grave.

If I was tickled by the lover's rub
That wipes away not crow's-foot nor the lock
Of sick old age upon the falling jaws:
Time and the crabs and the sweethearting crib
Would leave me cold as butter for the flies:
The biting days would soften as I struck
Bells on the dead fools' toes.

This world is half the devil's and my own,
Daft with the drug that's smoking in a girl
And curling round the bud that forks her eye.
An old man's shank one-marrowed with my bone,
And all the herrings smelling in the sea,

I sit and watch the worm beneath my nail
Wearing the quick away.

And that's the rub, the only rub that tickles.
The knobbly ape that swings along his sex
From damp love-darkness and the nurse's twist
Can never raise the midnight of a chuckle,
Nor when he finds a beauty in the breast
Of lover, mother, lovers or his six
Feet in the rubbing dust.

And what's the rub? Death's feather on the nerve?
Your mouth, my love, the thistle in a kiss?
My Jack of Christ born thorny on the tree?
The words of death are dryer than his stiff,
My wordy wounds are printed with your hair.
I would be tickled by the rub that is:
Man be my metaphor.

April 30, '34.

Collateral Poems

There exist a handful of poems that do not find a place in the previous sections, yet are of this period and should be available to those interested in Thomas's early development. The first two poems, found in manuscript, give indications of being drafts that, for some reason or other, failed to be entered into the *1930–1932 Notebook*. Others are early publications that were never in notebooks, or were possibly torn out. Others are revisions of notebook poems, standing intermediate between the first version and the later published poem. The last poem is based closely on an early poem now lost.

(1)

I have not moulded this marble
With my alabaster hands,
Nor formed it from your breasts,
But Lapitha made it for me, for a poem.

    Lapitha, I am your garment,
    Your bed, your wine showered with snow;
    There are voices about me, but my voice is a voice
    among voices, the greatest being yours, my
    Lapitha flower, my dicebox.

My mother was a marble harlot,
And my father feasted from her alabaster limbs,
Therefore pardon me, my Lapitha, my soul,
For the marble is moulded with a delicacy,
while my poem is fire, flame
with me, flame
with me.
Lapitha, Lapitha, dusk voice and dicebox,
My queen of the pagodamyth,
      are you my marble?
No, not even my alabaster.

(2)

    Calling temerity to see,
    Do, like my friends,
    Your bidding not by look or touch –
    Under, the will
    That makes them win.
    Surrender in grace,
    The impregnable,
    Not-to-be-taken
    By any, be they fair as any,

Now, then (no time,
            yet look to time) –
I'm negative,
At every point you scorn to be.
Why regularity?

(3)

You too have seen the sun a bird of fire
Stepping on clouds across the golden sky,
Have known man's envy and his weak desire,
Have loved and lost.
You, who are old, have loved and lost like I
All that is beautiful but born to die,
Have traced your patterns in the hastening frost.
And you have walked upon the hills at night,
And bared your head beneath the living sky,
When it was noon have walked into the light,
Knowing such joy as I.
Though there are years between us, they are nought;
Youth calls to age across the tired years:
'What have you found', he cries, 'what have you sought?'
'What you have found' age answers through his tears,
'What you have sought'.

(4)

That Sanity Be Kept

That sanity be kept I sit at open windows,
Regard the sky, make unobtrusive comment on the moon,
Sit at open windows in my shirt,
And let the traffic pass, the signals shine,

The engines run, the brass bands keep in tune,
For sanity must be preserved.

Thinking of death, I sit and watch the park
Where children play in all their innocence,
And matrons, on the littered grass,
Absorb the daily sun.

The sweet suburban music from a hundred lawns
Comes softly to my ears. The English mowers mow and mow.

I mark the couples walking arm in arm,
Observe their smiles,
Sweet invitations and inventions,
See them lend love illustration
By gesture and grimace.
I watch them curiously, detect beneath the laughs
What stands for grief, a vague bewilderment
At things not turning right.

I sit at open windows in my shirt,
Observe, like some Jehovah of the west,
What passes by, that sanity be kept.

(5)

That the sum sanity might add to nought
And words fall crippled from the slaving lips,
Girls take to broomsticks when the thief of night
Has stolen the starved babies from their laps,
I would enforce the black apparelled cries,
Speak like a hungry parson of the manna,
Add one more nail of praise on to the cross,
And talk of light to a mad miner.
I would be woven a religious shape;
As fleeced as they bow lowly with the sheep,
My house would fall like bread about my homage;

227

And I would choke the heavens with my hymn
That men might see the devil in the crumb
And the death in a starving image.

(6)

Do you not father me, nor the erected arm
For my tall tower's sake cast in her stone?
Do you not mother me, nor, as I am,
The lover's house, lie suffering my stain?
Do you not sister me, nor the erected crime
For my tall turrets carry as your sin?
Do you not brother me, nor, as you climb,
Adore my windows for their summer scene?
Do you not foster me, nor the hailfellow suck,
The bread and wine, give for my tower's sake?

Am I not father, too, and the ascending boy,
The boy of woman and the wanton starer
Marking the flesh and summer in the bay?
Am I not sister, too, who is my saviour?
Am I not all of you by the erected sea
Where bird and shell are babbling in my tower?
Am I not you who fronts the tidy shore,
Nor roof of sand, nor yet the towering tiler?
Am I not all of you, nor the hailfellow flesh,
The fowl of fire and the towering fish?

This was my tower, sir, where the scaffolded coast
Walls up the hole of winter and the moon.
Master, this was my cross, the tower Christ.
Master the tower Christ, I am your man.
The reservoir of wrath is dry as paste;
Sir, where the cloudbank and the azure ton
Falls in the sea, I clatter from my post
And trip the shifty weathers to your tune.
Now see a tower dance, nor the erected world
Let break your babbling towers in his wind.

(7)

Foster the light, nor veil the feeling moon,
Nor sister globes that fall not on the bone,
But strip and bless the marrow in the spheres;
Master the night, nor spite your starry spine,
Nor muster worlds that course not through the skin,
But know the clays that burrow round the stars.

Murmur of spring, nor crush the roaring eggs,
Nor hammer back the season in the figs,
But wind the summer-bearer in your get;
Farmer the wilds, nor fill the corny bogs,
Nor harm a weed that wars not in your legs,
But set and grow a meadow in the heart.

Move you unmarrowed in your ragged shifts,
O sea and sky, nor sorrow as this flesh
Goes from another with a nitric smile;
Nor as my bones are bridled on her shafts,
Nor when my locks are shooting in the turf,
Shall grief go salty-lidded in the gales.

One gave the clouds their colours and their shapes;
One gave me clay, and dyed the crowded sea
With the green wings of fish and flying men.
Set you your waves and daylights on my lips,
Give me your tempers and your tides as I
Have grafted flesh on to the sea and sun.

(8)

First I knew the lamb on knocking knees,
The ousel and the maniac greens of spring,
Caught on a narrow easel metal skies,
And on a yard of canvas inch of wing,
Kingfisher's, gull's swooping feather and bone,
Goodnight and goodmorning of moon and sun.

Redkneed tomboy ousted ousel and lamb;
Morning was saffron; and pink in the clouds
Rose a pound of fair breast; I was dumb
To say how divine were the woman moon's moods,
And how blithe the stars as they lay
Love scars on the woman of the sky.

(9)

Your breath was shed
Invisible to make
About the soiled undead
Night for my sake,

A raining trail
Intangible to them
With biter's tooth and tail
And cobweb drum,

A dark as deep
My love as a round wave
To hide the wolves of sleep
And mask the grave.

Notes

Abbreviations

Letters   *The Collected Letters of Dylan Thomas* ed. Paul Ferris (J. M. Dent 1985).

Collected   Dylan Thomas *Collected Poems 1934–1952* (J. M. Dent 1952), now re-edited in a definitive edition by Walford Davies and Ralph Maud *Collected Poems 1934–1953* (J. M. Dent 1988).

notebooks   *The Notebooks of Dylan Thomas* ed. Ralph Maud (New York: New Directions 1967); British edition, *Poet in the Making* (J. M. Dent 1968); now re-edited by Ralph Maud as the present volume, Dylan Thomas *The Notebook Poems 1930–1934* (J. M. Dent 1989).

18 Poems   Dylan Thomas *18 Poems* (*Sunday Referee* & Parton Bookshop 1934).

Twenty-five Poems   Dylan Thomas *Twenty-five Poems* (J. M. Dent 1936).

The Map of Love   Dylan Thomas *The Map of Love* (J. M. Dent 1939).

Deaths and Entrances   Dylan Thomas *Deaths and Entrances* (J. M. Dent 1946).

ed. Tedlock   *Dylan Thomas: The Legend and the Poet* ed. E. W. Tedlock (London: Heinemann 1960).

Texas   Harry Ransom Humanities Research Center, University of Texas, Austin, Texas.

Buffalo   The Poetry/Rare Books Collection, University Libraries, SUNY at Buffalo.

"Poetic Manifesto"   facsimile of the Thomas Manuscript in *Texas Quarterly* (Winter 1961) pp. 45–52, reprinted in Dylan Thomas *Early Prose Writings* ed. Walford Davies (J. M. Dent 1971) pp. 154–160.

231

Note: In this edition, as in the *Collected Poems 1934–1953*, the poems are printed so that a stanza break does not coincide with the bottom of a page unless the regular stanzaic pattern makes it obvious.

EARLY RHYMED VERSE

Juvenilia from Manuscripts

"The Mishap" & "The Maniac"

When Kent Thompson transcribed nine early manuscript poems as an appendix to his dissertation *Dylan Thomas in Swansea* (Swansea 1965), the originals were in the possession of Mrs Ken (Hettie) Owen, who had been given them by Thomas's mother when the two of them had discovered the papers in cleaning out a cupboard in Blaen Cwn cottage, Llangain, where Thomas had left them years before. The documents are now at the Harry Ransom Humanities Research Center, Texas. Paul Ferris gave a sample of them in his biography *Dylan Thomas* (1977).

"The Mishap"   [c. 1927]

The poem is signed 'Dylan Marlais', but the handwriting does not appear to be Thomas's. Kent Thompson thinks that Dylan's sister, Nancy, copied out the poem with a view to submitting it to a magazine such as the *Boy's Own Paper*. These remarkable verses capture the deadpan drollery of Hilaire Belloc's *Cautionary Tales*.

"The Maniac"   [c. 1929]

This poem in Thomas's hand, and in an accomplished late-eighteenth-century style, presages the theme of the mad Ophelia in such stories as "The Mouse and the Woman" and such poems as "Love in the Asylum".

"Song to a Child at Night-time"   [c. 1930]

This lullaby exists in a manuscript in Thomas's hand among manuscripts of other early poems at Texas.

"You hold the ilex by its stem"   [c. 1931]

This poem from a typescript in the British Library is dated by the internal evidence of style.

Verse from *Swansea Grammar School Magazine*

"A Ballad of Salad"   July 1929

Thomas was fourteen-and-a-half when he published this witty poem in his
school magazine. The London weekly *Everyman* had had a competition on
this theme the previous April; no doubt Thomas had submitted this poem,
though he did not earn a mention (as he did in the October 1929 competition).
This pastiche draws most obviously on Keats and Marvell.

"Request to an Obliging Poet"   April 1930

This light-hearted doggerel utilizes actual Welsh place-names in a way that
Thomas was not to do again until *Under Milk Wood*.

Sitwellian fashion (l. 9): Thomas had written in his essay "Modern Poetry"
published in the previous school magazine (December 1929): 'The position
of the Sitwells in poetical art is indefinite, only because they are curiously
regarded as obscurists, while a closer examination of their work cannot fail
to impress the mind with images and thoughts of a new and astonishing
clarity.'

"In Borrowed Plumes"   April 1930

This imitation of W. B. Yeats's early style was the second of two parodies on
the theme of 'Little Miss Muffet'. The first told of the intrusion of the spider
as Ella Wheeler Wilcox might have handled it. Parody was a common genre
of the time; Thomas might have seen, for instance, *Parrot Pie* by William
Kean Seymour of *Punch*, published in 1927.

"The Sincerest Form of Flattery"   July 1931

This contribution to the school magazine (Dylan was now editor) was 'A
Literary Course', with parodies of the Russian novel, Osbert Sitwell, Siegfried
Sassoon, a contemporary drama, and, lastly, 'the sentimental sonnet'.

"The Callous Stars"   July 1931

The image at the end of this poem of the sky weeping itself into darkness is
reminiscent of one of Thomas's last poems, the unfinished 'In Country
Heaven', where God weeps in sympathy with the self-destroyed Earth: 'Light
and His tears dewfall together'.

"Two Decorations"   July 1931

In *My Friend Dylan Thomas* (1977) Daniel Jones describes how he and Thomas
collaborated on poems, writing alternate lines, Jones the first line and sub-

233

sequent odd-numbered lines, Thomas the even-numbered. The original manuscripts of these collaborative poems can now be examined in the Humanities Research Center, Texas. There are numerous slips of paper containing poems in the two hands, and there are three exercise-books where the poems were written up by Jones, entitled: "Voiceless Frolic by Walter Bram"; "These Vines of Star – Walter Bram"; and "Poems by Walter Bram pseud." The first of the "Two Decorations" is poem XIX in the latter exercise-book. It should therefore be considered a collaboration, even though published over the initials D. M. T. in the school magazine. It was typed out by Thomas for submission to publishers along with several other "They" collaborations, now in the British Library and published in the Appendix to *Poet in the Making*.

The second of the "Two Decorations" is not included in the Texas holdings nor in the British Library typescripts. It is, however, no different in style from the other collaborative poems, and should be taken as a collaboration also.

Poems from the story, "The Fight"

"Frivolous is my hate"	[c. 1930]
"Warp"	[c. 1930]
"The Grass Blade's Psalm"	[c. 1930]

In the story from *Portrait of the Artist as a Young Dog* (1940) called "The Fight", the protagonist at the age of fourteen-and-three-quarters has already written many poems: 'I sat in my bedroom by the boiler and read through my exercise-books full of poems' (p. 77). He reads to Dan (an undisguised Dan Jones) from 'an exercise-book full of poems' (p. 83). Three poems quoted in full in the story are included here. There is a slight tone of self-mockery in the way they are brought into the story, and we cannot be absolutely certain that the titles and the poems themselves were not made up later, expressly for the story. However, they are presented in context as genuine poems of the period.

Rhymed Poems Deleted from the *1930 Notebook*

"One has found a delicate power"   [May 1930]

This was poem 9 in the notebook, but was deleted soon after being copied in. It is similar in style to the "They" series (e.g. the "Two Decorations" above), but there is no manuscript evidence to suggest that it was a collaborative poem.

"The shepherd blew upon his reed"   [June 1930]

This was poem *12* in the notebook. Thomas's attitude to the school magazine is revealed in the fact that he chose to print this poem in the issue of July 1930, while at the same time discarding it from the notebook. He gave it the fashionable title "Orpheus" in the magazine.

"The Shepherd to his Lass"   17 June 1930

Coming two poems after the previous poem *12* in the notebook, this poem also had the number *12* until it was deleted. In his piece "Children's Hour (or Why the B.B.C. Broke Down)" in the *Swansea Grammar School Magazine* December 1930, Thomas makes fun of this kind of pastoral lyric. In an imaginary tour of Arcadia, he has a Centaur sing:

> Pluck thy sportive lyre, O Chloe,
>   Charm the dolphins with its notes,
> Let the Tritons, soft and snowy,
>   Play upon their jocund oats...

However, Thomas liked this notebook poem well enough to write it in the autograph album of Bonnie L. James of Yr Hendre farm, St Dogmaels, North Pembrokeshire, when he stayed there for part of his summer holidays in 1930. The album is now in the National Library of Wales, Aberystwyth.

"The rod can lift its twining head"   [August 1930]

This was poem *30* in the notebook, before deletion.

1930 NOTEBOOK

1 "He stands at the steaming river's edge"   27 April 1930

Osiris, Come to Isis (title): Thomas probably had a specific source for his allusions to the Osiris–Isis story of Egyptian mythology. If that source were known, it might account for some of the puzzling details, such as *sadr* (ll. 9 and 60) and *Ishah* (l. 95), which items are not included in the normal reference works.

Seb and Nut (l. 14): 'Osiris was the offspring of an intrigue between the earth-god Seb (Keb or Geb, as the name is sometimes transliterated) and the sky-goddess Nut' – J. G. Frazer *Osiris* p. 6.

Alexandrian chorus (l. 35): 'The chief centre of the worship of Serapis in Ptolemaic times was Alexandria' – E. A. Wallis Budge *The Gods of the Egyptians*

Vol. 2, p. 197. *Cotta* (l. 36) must have been a name associated with the ritual in Thomas's source.

You had no abortion ... Or bad birth-mark, or contortion (ll. 41 & 43): These two lines are deleted in the notebook.

Why were you born again in the belly of Apis (l. 45): The 'you' was missing from the line, and has been supplied editorially. Apis was believed to be Osiris incarnate.

Set (l. 54): The malicious brother of Osiris.

Seb's fair daughter (l. 65): Isis.

sistrum (l. 71): A stringed instrument played in the worship of Isis.

Serapis (l. 103): Osiris–Apis.

dog-faced (l. 112): Neither Osiris nor Isis is given a dog's face in Egyptian iconography.

2 "The lion-fruit goes from my thumb"   2 May 1930

Mother Goose (title): In the posthumously published "Poetic Manifesto" Thomas wrote: 'The first poems I knew were nursery rhymes, and before I could read them for myself I had come to love just the words of them, the words alone.' This notebook poem is a variation on 'Mary, Mary, quite contrary,' 'Tom, Tom, the piper's son,' Rapunzel and possibly other themes.

3 "Grant me a period for recuperation"   2 May 1930

Illusion (title): The title has the air of self-mockery, which the poem supports, up to a point.

old master (l. 11): Presumably a master at the school, conceivably Thomas's own father, the senior English teacher. But the implication of 'rowing' is unclear.

Ceres (l. 18): The goddess of harvest – not, however, the goddess of wild oats.

4 "You shall not despair"   6 May 1930

5 "My vitality overwhelms you"   10 May 1930

6 "And so the new love came at length"   17 May 1930

Lilith (l. 31): The vengeful wife Adam is fabled to have had before Eve. Thomas may have seen the reference in Dante Gabriel Rossetti's "Eden Bower".

7 "You collect such strange shapes"   18 May 1930

On Watching Goldfish (title): The title is a signal that we have here an Imagistic poem.

The fishes have an envy ... (ll. 11–14): Four lines deleted in the notebook.

8 "The lion, lapping the water"   [May 1930]

Thomas listed 'Lawrence (animal poems …)' as one of the influences to be seen in his early poems (*Letters* p. 297).

And restoring his vitality (l. 3): This and eight other lines (out of the twenty-one lines of this short poem) have been deleted in the notebook (viz. ll. 6–8, 14–18).

9 "I am aware of the rods"   [June 1930]

There are an additional fifteen lines in the notebook, but they are thoroughly crossed out, with the marginal command: 'Omit.' The last line was doubly deleted.

> I am aware of the sun
> Between the rain,
> Confident,
> With its dignity and loud fastidiousness
> Studying the earth.
> Why does it stand so urbane?
> It is a thing to wonder at,
> To stretch back the head and admire,
> So much to itself,
> So independent and vast,
> Like an animal
> Living in its freedom,
> Or a king
> In an alabaster palace,
> Sunday all the week.

10 "My river, even though it lifts"   [June 1930]

11 "The corn blows from side to side lightly"   18 June 1930

Giant-flower (last line): Deleted in the notebook, and the full-stop of the previous line changed to a comma.

12 "We will be conscious of our sanctity"   6 June [1930]

13 "I have come to catch your voice"   19 June [1930]

14 "My love is a deep night"   [June 1930]

15 "When your furious motion is steadied"   1 July 1930

237

16 "No thought can trouble my unwholesome pose"

                                            17 July [1930]

17 "The hill of sea and sky is carried"   20 July [1930]

18 "So I sink myself in the moment"   [July 1930]

19 "No, pigeon, I'm too wise"   8 August [1930]

20 "The cavern shelters me from harm"   11 August [1930]

Fine, bright stone (l. 16): Deleted in the notebook.

21 "Her woven hands beckoned me"   28 & 29 April 1929

Woman on Tapestry (title): Daniel Jones in the notes to *Dylan Thomas: The Poems* (p. 281) explains that his mother was a weaver who had had a one-woman show of her tapestries in London. A panel, six by four feet, hung in their house. It was called "The Garden of Eden"; and Jones feels that Thomas could have been thinking of its strange landscapes in writing this poem, especially ll. 28–30.

I have made an image ... (ll. 32–38): Seven lines deleted in the notebook.

He is a friend (l. 39): The 'He' is altered to 'She' in the notebook, and 'feminine' in the next line is deleted.

You shall comfort me ... with dry veins (ll. 44–57): These lines headed 'Continuation of Woman on Tapestry' have been inserted in the poem according to Thomas's instructions in the notebook. The 'You' is inconsistent with the rest of the poem; the passage perhaps was not really written as a continuation. *There will be a new bitterness ... the tent of its wings* (ll. 58–71): These lines represent a second continuation, and were a rewriting of three lines that had appeared earlier in the poem (after l. 23) but were thoroughly deleted there:

> Let me believe in the clean faith of the body,
> The sweet, glowing vigour,
> And the gestures of unageing love.

These three lines were tried again at the end of the original poem, but were again crossed out. Their sense is retained in the inserted lines.

22 "Pillar breaks, and mast is cleft"   [August 1930]

23 "It's light that makes the intervals"   [August 1930]

24 "Let me escape"   [September 1930]

25 "Oh, dear, angelic time – go on"   [September 1930]

Oh, dear, angelic time (l. 1): A typescript of this poem in the British Library alters the beginning to: 'O dear, angelic Time.'

I can't be happy ... (ll. 14–16): The last three lines were deleted in the notebook, and not included in the typescript.

26 "And the ghost rose up to interrogate"   [September 1930]

distract (l. 11): This word is 'detract' in the notebook; presumably Thomas meant 'distract'.

hundred-coloured stairs (l. 31): There is no indication in the notebook that the speech ends with this line, but the context suggests it.

mustard-bird (l. 46): Appears to be a made-up name.

27 "When I allow myself to fly"   [October 1930]

28 "Admit the sun into your high nest"   [October 1930]

29 "We sailed across the Arabian sea"   [October 1930]

Hassan's Journey (title): In his "Poetic Manifesto" piece, Thomas said that his juvenilia included 'some very bad Flecker.' This poem gets its hero's name and journey motif from James Elroy Flecker, but it is not indebted to that poet for its symbolic narrative style.

Aegis (l. 82): A shield. The Lady of the poem is considered a protectress.

30 "I know this vicious minute's hour"   3 November 1930

31 "Her voice is a clear line of light"   4 November 1930

Claudetta, You, and Me (title): This title, crossed out in the notebook, could possibly refer to three people, and therefore does not help to clarify the puzzling pronoun references in the poem.

lorette (l. 25): A brightly-coloured Australian parrot.

leman (l. 27): Usually a female lover, and presumably so here.

32 "Come, black-tressed Claudetta, home"   5 November 1930

33 "Cool, oh no cool"   [November 1930]

Master ... (ll. 14–18): Presumably these lies are spoken by the doll. Inverted commas and question mark have been added editorially.

34 "They brought you mandolins"   [November 1930]

more (l. 39): This word is 'or' in the notebook; but presumably 'more' was meant.

at last (l. 46): Presumably the speech ends at this point; inverted comma supplied.

35 "The air you breathe encroaches"   [November 1930]

This poem is deliberately unpunctuated. The British Library typescript follows the notebook in this regard.

36 "When all your tunes have caused"   [November 1930]

37 "Am I to understand"   [November 1930]

Written in a classroom (headnote): There are many anecdotes about Thomas's nonchalance in respect to his schoolwork; he was apparently bottom of the class in everything except English.
I loved her once ... (ll. 27–41): Fifteen lines deleted, with l. 33, 'Love was a tiny boy', doubly deleted.
This thought ... (last three lines): Lines deleted in the notebook.

38 "Hand in hand Orpheus"   [November 1930]

Though the typescript in the British Library capitalizes the beginning word of all the lines, and introduces some punctuation, the state of the poem in the notebook, which is preserved here, indicates something of the poet's mental condition as he wrote it, witness the extra three deleted lines, not present in the typescript, and thoroughly crossed out in the notebook:

> so I am getting drunk
> sense she has wings
> and is just as sane.

39 "I, poor romantic, held her heel"   22 November 1930

A British Library typescript of this poem has the title "Cabaret".
her (l. 15): The word is 'my' in the notebook; but presumably 'her' is meant.
raise (l. 20): The word is 'rise' in the notebook; it was emended to 'raise' in the British Library typescript.

40 "Oh! the children run towards the door"   [November 1930]

41 "Tether the first thought if you will"   [December 1930]

Gratifying my sensualities (l. 32): Omitted in the British Library typescript.
Look down (last line): Deleted in the notebook, and omitted in the typescript.

42 "How shall the animal"   9 December 1930

"How shall my animal" of *The Map of Love* and *Collected* was a revision of this notebook poem, a very thorough revision. Thomas told Watkins that he 'had worked on it for months' (*Letters* p. 287). He sent the finished poem to Watkins with a letter of 21 March 1938.

Philistine (l. 9): As used by Matthew Arnold, one who scorns culture. In the context of this poem, it possibly signifies a part of the poet's own dual sensibility.

I build a tower and I pull it down (l. 10): This line was circled by Thomas, probably in 1938. In a letter to Vernon Watkins of 21 March 1938 Thomas quotes it as an image for 'creative destruction, destructive creation' (*Letters* p. 278).

When sense says stop (l. 39): Originally this line ended with three dots as punctuation, which were deleted, and a semi-colon was written over them. This is probably where the question ends, so a question mark has been supplied editorially.

1930–1932 NOTEBOOK

I "This love – perhaps I overrate it"　　　　December 1930

II "Today, this hour I breathe"　　　　18 December 1930

Several phrases from this notebook poem were utilized in the "Today, this insect" of *Twenty-five Poems* and *Collected*. There is no manuscript of the revision, which was very thorough, producing what amounts to a new poem.

prey (l. 21): The notebook has 'pray'; presumably 'prey' was meant.

III "Sometimes the sky's too bright"　　　　19 December 1930

IV "Here is the bright green sea"　　　　28 December 1930

Thomas published this poem in the *Swansea Grammar School Magazine* April 1931 as the first of "Two Images". He later wrote 'Ugh' in the margin of the notebook.

V "My golden bird the sun"　　　　30 December 1930

The second of "Two Images" in *Swansea Grammar School Magazine* April 1931, this poem also received a marginal pejorative: 'Ogh.'

VI "Live in my living"　　　　[December 1930]

But live,　　　　*, (l. 15):* Thomas left a space between the two commas for a phrase that he never supplied.

241

VII "Rain cuts the place we tread"   2 January 1931

A legendary horse (l. 17): If Pegasus is meant, the subject of this poem may be poetic composition itself.

VIII "The morning, space for Leda"   20 January 1931

Leda (ll. 1 & 29): Leda was the Queen of Sparta loved by Zeus in the form of a swan. Yeats's volume *The Tower*, containing "Leda and the Swan", had been published in 1928.

IX "The spire cranes"   27 January [1931]

The revised version published in *The Map of Love* and *Collected* relies heavily on this notebook poem. The revision was not done in the notebook, nor in any other extant manuscript. In sending the revision to Vernon Watkins on 13 November 1937, Thomas said: 'I've done another little poem: nothing at all important, or even (probably) much good: just a curious thought said quickly' (*Letters* p. 264).

X "Cool may she find the day"   [February 1931]

XI "Yesterday, the cherry sun"   22 February 1931

XII "Time enough to rot"   24 February [1931]

XIII "Conceive these images in air"   20 March [1931]

XIV "You be my hermaphrodite in logic"   24 March [1931]

XV "Until the light is less"   28 March [1931]

XVI "The neophyte, baptized in smiles"   6 April 1931

There seems to be no connection between this poem and the later "Then was my neophyte" – except for the word 'neophyte'.

acritudes (l. 23): A rare word meaning the same as 'acridities' (bitterness).

XVII "To be encompassed by the brilliant earth" 10 April 1931

wax's tower (l. 10): A phrase used later in sonnet VI of "Altarwise by owl-light".

XVIII "Who is to mar"   18 May 1931

There is similar imagery and theme in poem "Twenty Nine" of the *February*

1933 Notebook, the first draft of "We lying by seasand".

XIX "The natural day and night"   30 March 1931
This poem is entered in the notebook out of sequence, or Thomas accidentally wrote 'March' instead of 'May'. The poem seems to have been written impetuously, yet it was one of those chosen to be typed up for submission to editors (typescript in British Library).

corrupting (l. 30): The notebook word is 'incorruptible', but the British Library typescript has the preferable 'corrupting'.

XX "Although through my bewildered way"   1 June 1931

XXI "High on a hill"   1 June 1931

XXII "Refract the lady, drown the profiteer"   [June] 1931

XXIII "Into be home from home"   10 June [1931]
In a press release announcing a proposed new Swansea magazine *Prose and Verse*, Thomas said of contributions that 'their only qualification must be originality of outlook and expression' – quoted in *South Wales Daily Post* 2 June 1931. The notebook poems of around this date, including this one, are of a particularly forced originality.

Etching the mossy castle ... (l. 22): Line deleted in the notebook.

XXIV "if the lady from the casino"   16 June 1931
The point of this poem seems to be its spontaneity – contrasting with the title of the next poem.

XXV "Through sober to the truth"   3 July 1931

XXVI "It is the wrong, the hurt, the mineral"   28 July 1931

XXVII "Even the voice will not last"   2 August 1931
Thomas crossed out helpful commas at the end of ll. 1, 11, 12, and 14. He apparently wanted a poem without commas. There is an extra line to the poem in the notebook: 'These words come too easily.' It was possibly a comment on the poem. Thomas later deleted it thoroughly.

Glaucus (l. 27): A Greek god of the sea.
Pan and pot (l. 28): The Greek god of the wilds is linked here, by means of a pun, with a common kitchen utensil.

243

XXVIII "True love's inflated"   8 August 1931

XXIX "Since, on a quiet night, I heard them talk"
      12 August 1931

XXX "They are the only dead"   16 August [1931]

XXXI "Have hold on my heart utterly"   [August 1931]

hold (l. 1): The word is 'old' in the notebook; but presumably 'hold' was meant.

XXXII "The caterpillar is with child"   January 1931

The word 'Fragment' was written above the poem, probably referring to the first nine lines, which had a demarcation line after them. The line, and the word 'Fragment', were crossed out, and the poem was continued. Perhaps the date 'January 1931' refers to the nine lines, and the rest of the poem was composed in August 1931, in sequence.

Pierrot ... Toby ... Punch (ll. 15–16): A clown figure, like the Pierrot of French mime, is sometimes found with Toby the dog and Punch in Punch and Judy shows.

XXXIII "Foot, head, or traces"   18 August 1931

A typescript in the British Library has the title "Little Problem," and has several variants.

foot or head (l. 4): Became 'foot on head' in the typescript.
toe or foot (l. 12): Became 'toe of hair' in the typescript.
But plumb ... (last two lines): Were recast in the typescript as:

> But only plumb such depths
> As you, Original, derive.

XXXIV "When you have ground such beauty down to dust"
      [August 1931]

This poem is crossed out in the notebook, with a note: 'further in book'. The poem is found repeated verbatim as XLVII later, where the present edition places it.

XXXV "Or be my paramour or die"   [August 1931]

XXXVI "The womb and the woman's grave"   [August 1931]

XXXVII "Let Sheba bear a love for Solomon" [September 1931]
Sheba ... Solomon (l. 1): Well-known Biblical figures, but the poem does not appear to have a Biblical setting.

XXXVIII "There was one world and there is another"
[September 1931]

XXXIX "For us there cannot be welcome"
11 September [1931]

XL "An end to substance in decay's a sequence"
11 September [1931]

XLI "Why is the blood red and the grass green"
12 September [1931]
The theme of unanswerable questions is taken up again in a similar way in poem "Thirty Seven" of the *February 1933 Notebook*, the first draft of "Why east wind chills".

Job's voice ... Israel's (l. 7): The reference to Job, if not Israel, is apt, since Job is an Old Testament book concerned with seeking answers.

XLII "Have cheated constancy"   21 September 1931

XLIII "There's plenty in the world that doth not die"
24 September 1931
no misgiving (l. 6): Became 'great misgiving' in a British Library typescript of this poem.

XLIV "This time took has much"   30 September 1931

XLV "Which of you put out his rising"   15 October [1931]
Left it among the cigarette-ends ... (l. 8): this line is used again later in this notebook in an unnumbered poem, "Nearly summer, and the devil".

XLVI "Feeding the worm"   17 October 1931
A possible source is, "To Tirzah", in Blake's *Songs of Experience*, which Thomas knew well:

> Thou Mother of my Mortal part,
> With cruelty didst mould my Heart...

245

Didst close my Tongue in senseless clay,
And me to Mortal Life betray.

XLVII "When you have ground such beauty down to dust"
10 October 1931

This poem, with exactly the same wording, was entered into the notebook in August 1931 as poem "XXXIV".

XLVIII "Sever from what I trust"   July 1931

Thomas's note in the margin, 'Poem lost and then found', indicates how a poem of July 1931 comes to be included with poems of October 1931. There is an even earlier first draft, dated 29 April 1931, written in the fly-leaf of Thomas's copy of Osbert Sitwell's *Argonauts* (1927), now in the Humanities Research Center, Texas. (Square brackets indicate deletions.)

Sever from what I trust
The things, this time, I love,
Death, and the the shy entanglement of sense
Crying for age
To [change] [sanctify] bless its sad sobriety;
[Martyr, it cannot hope for more;]
It's blind, and out of tune,
Moving [as lines] symmetrically in chaos
Day through
Till we're all older, [wiser,]
[And alert to seasons]
Wise to the seasons' touch on us
Of hope, and time, and sun.
Death out of sense.
Then what I trust I love,
And, [with a look careful,] careless child again,
See your wise smile

April 29th '31

XLIX "Never to reach the oblivious dark"   26 October [1931]

one who is to die (l. 28): Thomas once said, 'I am always very ill' (*Letters* p. 9). His mother, in an interview with Colin D. Edwards, said that Thomas was, as a young boy, 'extremely delicate': 'when he was about fifteen he had a haemorrhage rather badly.' This notebook poem was written on the day before the poet's seventeenth birthday.

L "So that his philosophy be proven"   October [1931]

The title, "Introductory Poem", perhaps indicates that Thomas intended to use this poem as a preface to a volume.

Thus I defy ... (ll. 5–6): Lines deleted in the notebook. The 'I' was interlined over a 'we'.

LI "Take up this seed"   [October 1931]

LII "There in her tears were laughter and tears again"
          3 November 1931

LIII "How can the knotted root"   5 & 6 November 1931

LIV "Children of darkness got no wings"   October [1931]

Trevor Hughes (in a typescript at Buffalo) tells that when he first met him, Dylan and his sister Nancy were listening to a gramophone record she had just bought. It was a Negro Spiritual sung by Paul Robeson: 'It's me, it's me, O Lord,/Standing in the need of prayer.'

LV "It's not in misery but in oblivion"   March 1931

A poem out of sequence, written earlier in the year.

Oblivion is so loverless (l. 28): This line was repeated almost exactly in poem "XXIX".

LVI "What lunatic's whored after shadow"   November 1931

LVII "Here is a fact for my teeth"   [December 1931]

Probably an unfinished poem; the poet left the next page of the notebook blank.

LVIII "Any matter move it to conclusion"   January 1932

levity/Brevity poetry (ll. 13–14): Thomas deleted the original commas after these three words; he apparently wanted the poem without commas.

LVIV "Too long, skeleton, death's risen"   20 January 1932

Clean as a whistle (l. 6): Became 'Sly as an adder' in a typescript now in the British Library.

Take now content ... (ll. 7–8): Thomas quoted these lines from the notebook, or remembered them verbatim, in a letter to Trevor Hughes two years later in January 1934 (*Letters* p. 162).

247

whose breast hangs low (l. 11): Became 'whose blood runs thick' in the typescript.

LVV "No man knows loveliness at all"   April 1932

This poem is written after about a ten-week gap. Writing to Trevor Hughes on about 14 February 1932, Thomas had said: 'My purple is turning, I think, into a dull gray. I am at the most transitional period now. Whatever talents I possess may suddenly diminish or may suddenly increase. I can, with great ease, become an ordinary fool' (*Letters* p. 7). The first poem entered into the notebook after that statement is this beautiful lyric.

LVVI "Do thou heed me, cinnamon smelling"   April 1932

LVVII "They said, tired of trafficking"   5 May 1932

eaten (last line): Was 'riddled', which was deleted. Then 'eaten' was crossed out in turn; but no other adjective was supplied.

LVVIII "Be silent let who will"   May 1932

LVVIV "Being but men, we walked into the trees"
     7 May 1932

LVVV "The hunchback in the park"   9 May 1932

It is a poem ... (l. 22): Line crossed out in the notebook.
And the hunchback smiles (last line): Deleted, and the previous line's comma altered to a full-stop.

There is a REVISION of this poem on the opposite page of the notebook. It is similar to the final version published in *Deaths and Entrances* and *Collected*, but it has a few interesting variants. Parentheses in the following transcription indicate words circled in the text, with marginal alternatives. Square brackets indicate deleted words.

> The hunchback in the park
> A solitary mister
> Propped between trees and water
> From the opening of the garden lock
> That let the trees and water enter
> Until the (church-black) bell at dark (Sunday sombre)
> Eating bread from a newspaper
> Drinking water from the chained cup
> That the children filled with gravel

In the fountain basin where I sailed my ship
Slept at night in a dog kennel
But nobody chained him up.
Like the park birds he came early
Like the water he sat down
And mister they called hey mister
The (mitching) boys from the town (truant)
Running when he had heard them clearly
[Past lake and rockery]
On out of sound [.]
Past lake and rockery
Laughing when he shook his paper
Through the (Indian ambush) of the willow groves ([wild] loud zoo)
Hunchbacked in mockery
Dodging the park keeper
With his stick that picked up leaves.

And the old dog sleeper
Alone between nurses and swans
While the boys among willows
Made the tiger jump out of their eyes
[Apes – danced] To roar on the rockery stones
And The groves were blue with sailors

Made all day until bell time
A woman figure without fault
Straight as a young elm
Straight and tall from his crookèd bones
That she might stand in the night
After the lock and chains

All night in the unmade park
After the railings and shrubberies
The birds the grass the trees and the lake
Had followed the hunchback
And the wild boys innocent as strawberries
To his kennel in the dark.

This revised poem is dated July 1941, the last revision made in the notebooks before Thomas offered them for sale.

LVVVI "Out of the sighs a little comes"   7 June [1932]

This notebook poem came to form the first two stanzas of "Out of the sighs" as published in *Twenty-five Poems* and *Collected*. No revising was actually done in the notebook; the changes are minimal. The remaining two stanzas of the published poem were taken from "Were that enough", the last unnumbered poem of the notebook, below.

And that is true after ... (l. 9): Deleted in the notebook, but appears in the published poem.

split (l. 15): Becomes 'spilt' in the published version.

[unnumbered] "Here is a beauty on a bough"   [June 1932]

[unnumbered] "At last, in hail and rain"   May [1932]

The REVISION of this poem took place soon after it was first entered in the notebook, and is also dated 'May'. The first ten lines are revised by interlinear emendation. The last five lines are crossed out completely, and rewritten on the next page as seven new lines. The revised poem can be transcribed as follows. (Square brackets indicate deleted words.)

> At last, in hail and rain,
> The family failings lose the gain
> Made by these ten years' loving: –
> Enterprise, humility, and devildom
> All graveward of the hailstoned skies.
>
> Wind blew the man down
> Who could not stand such strain,
> For love to live is [love] work to die,
> And labour's lost in venom.
>
> The outrageous boy has found his master;
> The [rake] rage on holiday
> But now all every day
> Master goes prancing from a family malady
> [Smiling with slut and cigarette,]
> Going no place how well he knows
> And all dressed up in [sable] old skins with a pride
> For [Sheba, forbear] [moloch] forbear, outrager, and the rest.

The poem remained unpublished.

[unnumbered] "Upon your held-out hand"   25 June 1932

the new asylum (l. 18): Cefn Coed Hospital had just been built about a mile from Cwmdonkin Drive. 'We have a new asylum,' says Thomas in a letter of July 1933 to Trevor Hughes in London. 'It leers down the valley like a fool, or like a snail with the two turrets of its water towers two snails' horns' (*Letters* pp. 18–19).

[unnumbered] "Nearly summer, and the devil"   April 1932

'The prince of darkness is a gentleman,' Thomas wrote to Trevor Hughes, echoing Coleridge. 'But his satanic convolutions and contradictions abide by no gentlemanly conditions' (*Letters* p. 12).

Pursed (l. 11): Became 'Poised' in the British Library typescript of this poem. *Leaves it among* ... (last line): Similar to a line in poem "XLV" earlier in this notebook.

[unnumbered] "How the birds had become talkative"

June 1932

Bruising (l. 5): Was 'Brusing' in the notebook. 'Bruising' seems the best emendation.

[unnumbered] "Were that enough"   1 July [1932]

These fourteen lines were typed out as a separate poem in the typescripts now in the British Library; but at some point they were tacked on to "Out of the sighs" ("LVVVI" above) to produce the "Out of the sighs" as published in *Twenty-five Poems* and *Collected*.

FEBRUARY 1933 NOTEBOOK

One   "Sweet as the comets' kiss night sealed" 1 February 1933

the comets' kiss (l. 1): Was 'a dog's kiss' before alteration. Later in the poem (l. 38), night is characterized as 'kind as a dog'.
Leah's hand ... *Rachel's head* (ll. 30–31): The names of Jacob's two wives seem to be used here without special Biblical reference. In his story "The Mouse and the Woman", Thomas used the phrase: 'slept with Rachel and woke with Leah'.
Unwholesome thoughts ... (ll. 36–37): Lines deleted in the notebook.

Two   "It is death though I have died"   2 February 1933

This poem bears some resemblance to "I dreamed my genesis" of *18 Poems* and *Collected*; but there is no evidence that it was actually utilized in the composition of the later poem.

251

Three   "Had she not loved me at the beginning"
[February 1933]

Had she not loved me ... (ll. 1–2): 'Used later in "The Mouse and the Woman"'
(Thomas's marginal note). That short story contains the sentence: 'Had she
not been in the beginning, there would have been no beginning.'
Seen heaven, known hell (l. 5): The phrase was deleted in the notebook.
Stirred, like a lizard, in my hair (l. 9): Altered to 'Braked, like a bat, on my
hair.'
I planted a rose ... (ll. 11–13): The last three lines were deleted. The next page
was torn out of the notebook; it presumably contained a continuation of this
poem.

Four   "Before the gas fades with a harsh last bubble"
6 February 1933

And the state falls ... (ll. 7–8): Two lines deleted in the notebook.
Man's manmade sparetime (l. 19): In this context Thomas is talking literally of
mass unemployment in Britain.

Five   "Hold on, whatever slips beyond the edge"
8 February 1933

loving thinking (l. 4): After this phrase, the poem as originally written con-
tinued with the following deleted lines:

grudge
Not others' trust, to trample not to dust
The others' closekept loves with merciless hooves.

There was a time I could cry (l. 11): A day or so before this poem was written,
Thomas had been given the news that his aunt Annie of Fernhill farm was
dying of cancer. In a letter to Trevor Hughes that day, Thomas is amazed at
his own anaesthetized emotions:

> Should I weep? Should I pity the old thing? For a moment, I feel, I should.
> There must be something lacking in me. I don't feel worried, or hardly
> ever, about other people. It's self, self, all the time. I'm rarely interested
> in other people's emotions, except those of my pasteboard characters. I
> prefer (this is one of the thousand contradictory devils speaking) style to
> life, my own reactions to emotions rather than the emotions themselves.
> Is this, he pondered, a lack of soul? (*Letters* p. 13).

A REVISION dated December 1935, written out on the opposite page of the
notebook, is identical to "Was there a time" as published in *Twenty-five Poems*

and *Collected*, except that 'maggots' (l. 4) became 'maggot' in the published version.

Six   "After the funeral, mule praises, brays" 10 February 1933

The other heads ... (l. 13): Though it is not exactly clear, Thomas seems to have intended to alter the line to read: 'The other masks, spy, mewling, on black books.'

little pain (l. 15): The notebook originally had an extra line, 'Wounded with a sharp sword', which was deleted, and is absent from the typescript of this poem in the British Library.

smile (l. 16): Was deleted, and 'stain' interlined.

joke (last line): Altered to 'dart', which was in turn deleted. As altered, the line would finally have read: 'Has dried like paint in the park sun.' This last line, and the notebook poem as a whole, has a cold satirical quality reminiscent of the letter Thomas wrote to Trevor Hughes on first hearing the news of his aunt's death:

> The odour of death stinks through a thousand books and in a thousand homes. I have rarely encountered it (apart from journalistic enquiries), and find it rather pleasant. It lends a little welcome melodrama to the drawing room tragicomedy of my most uneventful life. After Mother's departure I am left alone in the house, feeling slightly theatrical. Telegrams, dying aunts, cancer, especially of such a private part as the womb, distraught mothers and unpremeditated train-journeys, come rarely. They must be savoured properly and relished in the right spirit (*Letters* p. 13).

The anonymous 'him or her' of this notebook poem written immediately after the actual funeral becomes 'sculptured Ann' of "After the funeral (In memory of Ann Jones)" in *The Map of Love* and *Collected*. There is no extant manuscript of the revision process. Beneath the poem in the notebook Thomas wrote, and circled, the phrase: 'Birth of the womb'. This could have been done at the time of the revision in 1938.

Seven   "We who were young are old"   16 February 1933

hath (l. 3): Altered to 'has' in the notebook.

hearken (last line): Altered to 'listen'; then the whole line was deleted, and a full-stop supplied for the previous line. The deleted line was utilized in the last part of poem "Nine (Conclusion of Poem Seven)."

Eight   "To take to give is all"   [February 1933]

The poem may not be complete as it stands; the bottom half of the notebook page was torn off, possibly at the time of its revision. Thomas began revising the poem by alterations to the original text, as follows:

throwing manna (l. 2): Altered to 'blowing the quids'; the end comma was altered to a full-stop, and the next two lines deleted.

death (l. 5): the word 'dirt' was interlined, then deleted.

at last (l. 6): the end comma was deleted, and an extra line added: 'All currencies of the marked breath'.

The REVISION on the opposite page of the notebook, dated 'Laugharne. Sept. 1938', begins with three lines indicating the setting:

> For three lean months now, no work done
> In summer Laugharne among the cockle boats
> And by the castle with the boatlike birds

This opening was discarded, and a new start was made, which became the first two stanzas of "On no work of words" as published in *The Map of Love* and *Collected*. Two lines then follow:

> To take to leave from the richness of man is pleasing death;
> Unpleasant death will rake at last all currencies of the marked breath.

These two lines were immediately recast as the first two lines of a revision which proceeds as in the final two stanzas of the published "On no work of words".

Nine   "No faith to fix the teeth on carries"   17 February 1933

Harlem, Bedlam, Babel, and the Ghetto (l. 23): Thomas draws on New York's black district, the London mental hospital, the multilingual tower of Genesis, and the Near Eastern slums in order to make his point about universal suffering.

Piccadilly men (l. 24): Pimps or others frequenting London's nightclub district.

listening to the air (l. 38): Was, before alteration, 'hearkening to the wind' as in the last line of poem "Seven" above. Various echoes towards the end of this poem bear out that it is, as a note says, the 'Conclusion of Poem Seven'.

Ten   "Out of a war of wits"   22 February 1933

Called for confessor but there was none (l. 5): "Holy Spring" as published in *Deaths and Entrances* and *Collected* contains the line: 'Call for confessor but there was none'. A few other borrowed phrases indicate that this notebook poem was available to Thomas for the composition of "Holy Spring".

The sun shines strong . . . (ll. 12–13): Two lines deleted in the notebook.

fools' talk (l. 17): Was altered to 'friends' talk'. The scene in the poem is reminiscent of the evenings depicted in "Where Tawe Flows" in *Portrait of the Artist as a Young Dog*.

Eleven   "In wasting one drop from the heart's honey cells"
23 February 1933

Twelve   "With all the fever of the August months"
End of February 1933

Of every nature-writer from Fleet-street (l. 10): Line deleted in notebook.
horrible desires (l. 27): A striking phrase used later in "Then was my neophyte"
as published in *Twenty-five Poems* and *Collected*.

Thirteen   "Their faces shone under some radiance"
[February 1933]

Thomas tried "In Hyde Park" as a title for the poem, but then deleted it. It is
doubtful that he had yet visited London.

Fourteen   "I have longed to move away"   1 March 1933

The REVISION on the opposite page of the notebook is "I have longed to move
away" as published in *Twenty-five Poems* and *Collected*. It is dated 13 January
1936, by which time, of course, Thomas had moved away from Swansea.

Fifteen – missing from the notebook.

Sixteen   "The waking in a single bed"   22 March 1933

'My sister is soon to be married,' said Thomas in a letter to Trevor Hughes of
February 1933. Nancy's forthcoming marriage (which actually did not take
place until May) may have been in Thomas's mind in writing this poem.

The REVISION of this poem began with interlinear alterations to the original
text. These were mainly incorporated in the revised version written out on
the opposite page in the notebook:

For a Woman Just Married

> The waking in a single bed when light
> Struck luckily the palaces of her face
> And morning's sun trod true in the sky,
> (The last possessor), is gone forever,
> Her moonstruck self sold for one guest for good
> Who will disturb the cellars of her blood.
> Where there was one are two and nothing's shared
> Of love and light in all whole holy world
> Save that love-light of half love smeared
> Over the countenance of the bucking beast,
> And he, love knows, soon perishes the breast,

255

Reducing the midnight sun, for want of a wiser
Image on the ghost of paper,
Of single love to dust.

No longer
Will the vibrations of the sun desire on
Her deepsea pillow where once she sank alone,
Her heart all ears and eyes,
Lips catching the honey of the golden
Ghost small as a farthing
Hidden behind a cloud, for where
She lies another's secret at her side,
And through his circling arm she feels
The secret coursing of his undazzled blood.

It can be called a sacrifice. It can
With equal truth under the fled sun
Be called the turning of sun's love to man,
And now in the closed night
There can be no wild warming by sun's light.

Revised January 1941.

This revised poem was in turn subject to interlinear alterations:
the palaces of her face (l. 2): Altered to 'her mute, skyscraping face'; 'mute' was then altered to 'mazed'.
trod true in the sky (l. 3): Altered to 'rode proud out of her thighs'; 'proud' was then altered to 'like a sun', which was then altered to 'hard'.
sold (l. 5): Altered to 'razed'.
good (l. 5): An end full-stop was added, and the next line (l. 6) deleted.
whole holy (l. 8): Altered to 'the hot, sunless'.
Save the love-light (l. 9): Altered to 'But that blind shadow'.
breast (l. 11): Altered to 'ghost'.
honey (l. 19): Altered to 'avalanche'.
another's secret (l. 22): Altered to 'another lies'.
secret (l. 24): Altered to 'silent'.
fled sun (l. 26): Altered to 'deserted moon'.
closed (l. 28): Altered to 'double'.
sun's light (last line): Altered to 'sun light'.

There was a further thorough revision in July 1941 (not extant in any manuscript) before Thomas achieved the version published in *Deaths and Entrances* and *Collected* as "On the Marriage of a Virgin'. That title – incomplete as "On The Marriage Of A" – appears in the notebook, crossed out, as also does another title, "Dog-in-a-Manger", which may be an oblique comment on the subject of the poem.

Seventeen   "See, on gravel paths"   31 March 1933

Part of this poem (that is, all except ll. 31–58) was published by Thomas in *Herald of Wales* 8 June 1935, but not collected in any of his volumes. The last part of the poem, from 'See, on gravel paths', was quoted by Thomas in the BBC broadcast "Reminiscences of Childhood" as an example of poetry 'never to be published'.

Is the ripening of apples (l. 17): Line deleted, and 'Is' put at the beginning of the next line.
And a delicate confusion ... (l. 19): Line deleted.
There is no place ... (ll. 31–37): Seven lines deleted.
Whether from passing smiles ... (ll. 56–58): Three lines deleted.
There in the sunset ... (ll. 70–72): Three lines deleted.
Or the steeples ... *changing sky* (ll. 77–78): Deleted in notebook, with the next phrase capitalized: 'He is alone'.

Eighteen   "Make me a mask to shut from razor glances"
                                        [March 1933]

Deceiving each pretty miss ... (ll. 13–16): Four lines deleted. The following two lines were interlined in their place:
> Turning the bold wind sick, that shall deceive
> The treacherous heart and the squat lies.

The evil in ... (ll. 31–32): These two lines were altered to read:
> The evil squeezed through these two chinks in the sun
> Shall cheat the innocence behind the mask.

REVISION entered on the opposite page in the notebook was dated 'Nov 1937 Blashford'. Thomas was staying at his mother-in-law's house near Ringwood, Hants. The first nine lines of the original poem were utilized, to produce "O make me a mask" as published in *The Map of Love* and *Collected*.

Nineteen   "To follow the fox at the hounds' tails"
                                        28 March [1933]

Broken flank ... (l. 7): Line deleted in the notebook.
breaking/Butt-ends lying at dead-ends forsaken (ll. 22–23): Words deleted.
bed (l. 24): Thomas altered this to 'bad' in pencil in a typescript (Texas).
There is a smell ... (ll. 26–28): Last three lines were deleted.
Diana (l. 27): The Greek goddess of the hunt, not viewed favourably by the poet.

Twenty   "The ploughman's gone, the hansom driver"
                                        28 March 1933

257

hansom (l. 1): A two-wheeled covered horse-drawn carriage.
windmills (l. 6): Thomas acknowledges he is something of a Don Quixote in this nostalgic poem.
Beneath a balcony (ll. 13–15): Three lines deleted in the notebook.
Juliet (l. 14): None other than Romeo's beloved, discovered here in the waste land.

Twenty One   "Light, I know, treads the ten million stars"
1 April 1933

The poem in the notebook had an extra two lines:

> I am a timid child when day is sped,
> And my god is a child's god.

These lines were thoroughly deleted in the notebook, and were omitted in a typescript of this poem (Texas).
Hesperides (l. 2): The Western horizon.
turnip ghost (l. 5): Halloween mask.

Twenty Two   "My body knows its wants"   2 April 1933

the moon (l. 6): Words deleted in the notebook; 'my love' interlined.
A friend is but an enemy on stilts (l. 21): Thomas circled this line in the notebook, and used it later in "To Others than You", published in *Deaths and Entrances* and *Collected*.
Man's wants ... (ll. 26–29): The last four lines of this poem were deleted. They provided the beginning of "And death shall have no dominion", the next poem in the notebook.

Twenty Three   "And death shall have no dominion"
April 1933

This, the first poem in this notebook in regularly rhymed stanzas, was written in friendly competition with A. E. Trick to see who could write the best poem on the subject of Immortality. Thomas adapted the wording of Romans 6:9, 'Christ being raised from the dead dieth no more; death hath no more dominion over him.' Trick's attempt, entitled "For Death Is Not The End", appeared in the *Swansea and West Wales Guardian* 15 June 1934.

lie (l. 13): Deleted, and 'be laid' added interlinearly.

Thomas sent this original notebook poem to *New English Weekly*, where it was published 18 May 1933, his first poem in a respected London journal. The REVISION on the opposite page of the notebook was done later, in February 1936; it is as published in *Twenty-five Poems* and *Collected*.

Twenty Four   "Within his head revolved a little world"
16–20 April 1933

Probably submitted to *New English Weekly* with the previous poem, it was published there later, in the issue of 25 January 1934, with the title "Out of the Pit". It was not included by Thomas in any of his volumes.

scolecophidian (l. 22): Pertaining to a genus of snake.
through every hole (l. 26): Was, before alteration, 'from nose and arse".
Sanger's (l. 26): A well-known travelling circus of the time.

Twenty Five   "Not from this anger, anticlimax after"
20 April 1933

The REVISION entered on the opposite page of the notebook is the "Not from this anger" as published in *The Map of Love* and *Collected*. It is dated at Blashford January 1938. Thomas sent it to Vernon Watkins in March 1938; and after discussion on it (*Letters* p. 287) he went back to the notebook and changed the line that was 'In a land without weather' (l. 5) to 'In a land strapped by hunger', as it was finally published.

Twenty Six   "The first ten years in school and park"
22 April 1933

Harrow on the Hill,/The playing fields of Eton (ll. 12–13): An odd reference to the two most famous English public schools, later crossed out.
Height and depth ... (l. 27): Line deleted, and full-stop added to preceding line.
Toulouse (l. 47): A French radio station received in Britain.
Appreciation Hour ... (l. 48): A radio programme from the United States. The line was deleted in the notebook.
Ford ... Blue Bird ... Moth (ll. 58–59): The new mechanized world is here typified by a Ford tractor, Sir Malcolm Campbell's racing car 'Bluebird'. and the De Havilland two-seater plane, the 'Moth'.
Twenty years (l. 64): Thomas was eighteen when the poem was written.

Twenty Seven   "Pass through twelve stages"   23 April 1933

The centre leaves of the notebook came loose, and are missing. The first thirty-three lines of this poem are supplied from a British Library typescript made from the notebook in 1933.

Shall it be male or female? say the cells (l. 15) ... *As time on time sea ribbon rounds/Parched shires in dry lands* (ll. 27–28) ... *herring smelling* (l. 31): These phrases are utilized in poem "Forty One" in the *August 1933 Notebook*, which became the "If I were tickled by the rub of love" of *18 Poems* and *Collected*.
Round Robin (l. 46): A letter passed around for several people to sign.

259

Twenty Eight   "First there was the lamb on knocking knees"
13 May 1933

First there was the lamb on knocking knees (l. 1) ... *The black sheep, shuffling of the fold, old winter* (l. 33): These two lines appear in sonnet III of "Altarwise by owl-light" of *Twenty-five Poems* and *Collected*. An intermediate version is included in the 'Collateral Poems' section of the present volume.
ousel (ll. 2 and 39): Variant spelling of 'ouzel', a species of bird which includes the blackbird.

Twenty Nine   "We lying by seasand"   16 May 1933

The REVISION which appears on the opposite page of the notebook is a fair copy of the poem as it was published in *Poetry* (Chicago) January 1937 and later in *The Map of Love* and *Collected*. It was entered in the notebook on one of Thomas's return trips to Swansea, and dated from there September 1937. He left out the two lines beginning 'But wishes breed not' (ll. 21–22).

Thirty   "Incarnate devil in a talking snake"   16 May 1933

The title, "Before We Sinned", was added later, in pencil.
The revision of the poem took place outside the notebook; we have record of an intermediate version on a separate sheet of paper in the Buffalo collection:

> Incarnate devil in a talking snake,
> The central plains of Asia in his garden,
> In shaping time the circle stung awake,
> In shapes of sin forked out the old-horned fruits,
> And god walked there who was a fiddling warden
> And played down pardon from a tree of ghosts.
>
> When storms struck on the tree, the flying stars
> And the half moon half handed in a cloud
> Spread good and evil till the fancy fears
> All in a fret of weathers made a word,
> And when the moon came silently she was
> Half white as wool, and greener than the grass.
>
> We in our eden knew the eastern guardian
> In golden waters that no frost could harden
> And in our time that tumbled from the earth;
> He in a horn of sulphur and the cloven myth

There was further revision before the poem was published in the *Sunday Referee* 11 August. (It there had the title, "Poem for Sunday", which may have been chosen by the editor, Victor Neuburg.) This published REVISION was copied into the notebook on the opposite page, and dated 20 January 1936, with one variant: 'thunder's hill' of the periodical printing became 'heavens' hill' (l. 6), as found in the later printing in *Twenty-five Poems* and *Collected*.

Thirty One   "Now understand a state of being"   18 May 1933

Wish for the nevergift of dying (l. 24): This line was not deleted, but on the opposite page in the notebook Thomas made several attempts at rewriting it, ending with the alternative: 'Will long for death who's long in coming.'

Thirty Two   "Interrogating smile has spoken death"
20 May 1933

Thirty Three   "No man believes"   23 May 1933

The notebook poem was published in *Adelphi* September 1933, but not included by Thomas in any of his volumes.

No man believes/Who curses not what makes and saves (ll. 13–14): Thomas once spoke to an audience about his father's atheism, an atheism which

> had nothing to do with whether there was a god or not, but was a violent and personal dislike for God. He would glare out of the window and growl: "It's raining, blast Him!" or, "The sun is shining – Lord, what foolishness!" (ed. Tedlock p. 66).

Thirty Four – missing from the notebook.

Thirty Five   "When I lie in my bed and the moon lies in hers"
1 July 1933

A title, "Children's Song", was added in pencil. However, the whole poem was thoroughly crossed out in the notebook. The dedication 'For P.T.' was presumably to Bert Trick's young daughter, Pamela, who also has a connection with poem "Thirty Seven" below.

most fear him (l. 8): This phrase and the general tone of the song remind one of Thomas's later poem to his own daughter, "In Country Sleep".

Thirty Six   "The tombstone tells how she died"   July 1933

Catholic (l. 11): Deleted, and 'gold-eyed' interlined.
mirror inside (l. 12): Before alteration, the line ended with 'clean inside'. The 'clean' was deleted, and 'mirror' interlined, and the next line added interlinearly.

261

The REVISION on the opposite page of the notebook was dated 'Sept 1938. Laugharne'. (Deleted words are in square brackets.)

> The tombstone told when she died.
> Her two surnames stopped me still.
> A virgin married at rest.
> She married in this [raining] pouring place,
> That I struck one day by luck,
> Before I heard in my mother's side
> Or saw in the looking-glass shell
> The rain through her cold heart speak
> And the sun killed in her face.
> More the thick stone cannot tell.
>
> Before she lay on a stranger's [farmer's] bed
> With a hand plunged through her hair,
> Or that [small wet] raining tongue beat back
> Through the [small] devilish years and innocent [great] *deaths*
> To the room of a [quiet] secret child,
> Among men later I heard it said
> She cried her white-dressed limbs were bare
> And her red lips were kissed black,
> She wept in her pain and made *mouths*,
> Talked and tore though her eyes smiled.
>
> I who saw in a [hurried] [winding] hurried film
> Death and this mad *heroine*
> Met once on a mortal wall,
> Heard her speak through the chipped beak
> Of the [angel] stone bird guarding her:
> I died before bedtime came
> But my womb was *bellowing*
> And I felt with my bare fall
> A [strange and] blazing red harsh head tear up
> And the [great] dear floods of his hair.

In a letter of around 11 September 1938 Thomas asked Watkins about the last line of the revised poem: 'I'm not quite sure of several words, mostly of "great" floods of his hair. I think it's right, though; I didn't want a surprisingly strong word there. Do tell me about it, soon' (*Letters* p. 326). In his next letter, 14 October 1938, Thomas showed his thinking on several points of diction:

I considered all your suggestions most carefully. A 'strange & red' harsh head was, of course, very weak & clumsy, but I couldn't see that the alliteration of 'raving red' was effective. I tried everything, & stuck to the commonplace 'blazing', which makes the line violent enough then, if not exactly good enough, for the last. In the last line you'll see I've been daring, & have tried to make the point of the poem softer & subtler by the use of the dangerous 'dear'. The word 'dear' fits in, I think, with 'though her eyes smiled', which comes earlier. I wanted the girl's *terrible* reaction to orgiastic death to be suddenly altered into a kind of despairing love. As I see it now, it strikes me as very moving, but it may be too much of a shock, a bathetic shock perhaps, & I'd like very much to know what you think. No, I still think the womb 'bellowing' is allright, exactly what I wanted; perhaps it looks too much like a stunt rhyme with heroine, but that was unavoidable. 'Hurried' film I just couldn't see; I wanted it slow & complicated, the winding cinematic works of the womb. I agree with your objection to 'small'; 'innocent' is splendid, but 'fugitive' & 'turbulent' are, for me in that context, too vague, too 'literary' (I'm sorry to use that word again) too ambiguous. I've used 'devilish', which is almost colloquial (*Letters* pp. 327–328).

For a while Thomas preferred 'winding' to 'hurried' (l. 21); that word appears in the periodical publications, *Seven* Winter 1938 and *Poetry* (Chicago) November 1939. But he reverted to 'hurried' for publication in *The Map of Love* and *Collected*.

Thirty Seven　"Why east wind chills"　　　1 July 1933

What colour is glory? (l. 18): This question was asked by Pamela Trick (aged four) in Thomas's presence, and he wrote it down. It gave impetus to a redoing of poem "XLI", above, on the theme of the impossibility of knowing certainties about the world. This particular question was dropped when the poem was revised for publication, but was picked up again for use in "My world is pyramid" of *18 Poems* and *Collected*.
Where once a vulture ... (ll. 25–28): Four lines deleted in the notebook.
big with war (l. 46): Phrase deleted.

The REVISION entered on the opposite page of the notebook and dated 21 January 1936 is practically identical to "Why east wind chills", published in *Twenty-five Poems* and *Collected*, except that a line (l. 14 as published) was inadvertently dropped out of the fair copy written into the notebook.

Thirty Eight　"This is remembered when the hairs drop out"
4 & 5 July 1933

sixty (l. 31): Word deleted in the notebook, but no alternative supplied.
In the beginning/Was the word (ll. 34–35): Made much use of later, in poem "Fifteen" of the *August 1933 Notebook*, which became "In the beginning" of *18 Poems* and *Collected*.

Half is remembered ... (ll. 37–38): Thomas quoted these last two lines from the notebook in a letter to Pamela Hansford Johnson of 20 July 1934 (*Letters* p. 158), after she had apparently used the word 'teredo' (woodworm) in a letter to him.

Thirty Nine   "In me ten paradoxes make one truth" July 1933

This is one of the poems praised by Pamela Hansford Johnson, but considered by Thomas to be 'very bad indeed' (*Letters* p. 125).

Forty   "A woman wails her dead among the trees"

7 July 1933

The 'local paper' mentioned in Thomas's headnote to this poem was the *Herald of Wales*, where the poem appeared on 15 July 1933 entitled, "Greek Play in a Garden". In his autobiographical BBC broadcast "Return Journey", Thomas says: 'used to have poems printed in the *Herald of Wales*; there was one about an open-air performance of *Electra* in Mrs Bertie Perkins's garden in Sketty.' The play was produced by Thomas Taig on 5–6 July 1933; music by Daniel Jones. Ethel Ross in her reminiscence, "Dylan Thomas and the Amateur Theatre", *The Swan* (March 1958), writes: 'Dylan Thomas came along one evening. I remember seeing him, slightly apart from the audience, leaning against a tree, a cigarette hanging from his lips. He looked extremely bored. So much so that one of his former masters was heard to remark, "If Thomas can't look a little more appreciative he'd better stay away." ' In his story "The Mouse and the Woman", Thomas refers to the performance: 'There had been seven women, in a mad play by a Greek, each with the same face, crowned with the same hoop of mad, black hair. One by one they trod the ruler of turf, then vanished. They turned the same face to him, intolerably weary with the same suffering'.

Forty One   "Praise to the architects"   7 July 1933

Who steps on the gas (l. 9): Line deleted in the notebook.

pome (l. 11): A 'jocular version of the word "poem" often used by Thomas and his friends, sometimes satirically, as here, but more often with a kind of affectionate informality' – Daniel Jones, note in *Dylan Thomas: The Poems* p. 255.

Keatings (l. 12): Presumably a brand name.

Auden (l. 13): Thomas referred to Auden in a letter of January 1934: 'Does one need "New styles of architecture, a change of heart"? Does one not need a new consciousness of the old universal architecture and a tearing away from the old heart of the things that have clogged it?' (*Letters* p. 93). And further, in March 1934: 'the most recent poems of Auden and Day-Lewis seem to me to be neither good poetry nor propaganda. A good propagandist needs little intellectual appeal; and the emotional appeal in Auden wouldn't raise a corresponding emotion in a tick' (*Letters* p. 97).

Forty Two   "Here in this spring"   9 July 1933
Some revision was made interlinearly in the notebook poem; the changes were adopted in the REVISION entered on the opposite page, dated January 1936, which is the version published in *Twenty-five Poems* and *Collected*.

Forty Three   "A praise of acid or a chemist's lotion"
                                          9 July 1933
The poem was crossed out, but no attempt at revision was made.
Onan (l. 14): The Biblical figure who wasted his seed.

Forty Four   "Too many times my same sick cry"   9 July 1933
Again the poem crossed out, without revision.

Forty Five   "We have the fairy tales by heart"   14 July 1933
Eden (l. 10): Altered to 'garden' interlinearly.
garden (l. 11): Altered to 'evening' interlinearly.
gnomes (l. 30): Altered to 'characters' interlinearly.

Forty Six   "Find meat on bones"   15 July 1933
Doom on the sun (l. 40): In a letter of May 1934 Thomas considered this a good title for a novel he said he was writing (*Letters* p. 134).

The REVISION to this poem was done entirely interlinearly, then dated January 1936. The poem so amended is the text as published in *Twenty-five Poems* and *Collected*.

Forty Seven   "Ears in the turrets hear"   17 July 1933
John O'London's Weekly dropped the second stanza when it published this poem, entitled "Dare I?", on 5 May 1934. Thomas wrote to Pamela Hansford Johnson that the poem was 'a terribly weak watery little thing' (*Letters* p. 131). He passed over it for *18 Poems*, but included it in *Twenty-five Poems* and *Collected*.

Forty Eight   "No food suffices but the food of death" July 1933
The Woman Speaks (headnote): The poem was given this title when published in *Adelphi* March 1934. Thomas explained the situation to Pamela Hansford Johnson in a letter of September 1933: 'Incidentally, I'd better mention that the poem starting, "No food suffices", is, though complete in itself, the woman's lament from an unfortunately unfinished play. I think this needs

mention; references in the poem would otherwise cast aspersions on the nature of my sex' (*Letters* p. 22). A manuscript of the poem in the British Library indicates that the unfinished play was to have been called *Ravens*. Thomas intended to revise the poem for *18 Poems*, but he did not do so, and did not include it in any later collection.

Forty Nine – missing from the notebook.

Fifty   "Let the brain bear the hammering"   August 1933

Domdaniel (l. 6): 'Our words,' Thomas wrote in a letter of January 1934, 'are spells to drag up the personified Domdaniel pleasure. Everything we do drags up a devil' (*Letters* p. 161).

Beware the treaty and the gun (last line): This interlined line replaced the deleted line: 'His playmates play with heart and brain.'

Fifty One   "The minute is a prisoner in the hour" August 1933

First vision that set fire to the air (l. 6): The last word 'air' was deleted, and 'year' interlined, which was then deleted and 'stars' interlined. Though 'stars' was itself deleted in the notebook, it was not replaced, and appears in the line as used later, in "Love in the Asylum" of *Deaths and Entrances* and *Collected*: 'Suffer the first vision that set fire to the stars.'

Between the first and second stanzas Thomas wrote the unfinished line: 'You woke and the dawn spoke and the.' He referred to this fragment when writing to Vernon Watkins 1 April 1938: 'I've got one of those very youthfully-made phrases, too, that often comes to my mind and which one day I shall use: "When I woke, the dawn spoke"' (*Letters* p. 287). He used it, of course, in "When I woke" of *Deaths and Entrances* and *Collected*.

On the page opposite this poem in the notebook are two attempts at working on this poem. It could be revision, but it seems more likely, from internal evidence, to be preliminary drafting. (Square brackets indicate deleted words.)

> This minute's locked to learn me in the hour,
> [O] [And] Who sees it burn to break the chiming cell
> And play the truant in the den of days
>
> Chock   Loud   burn and break
>   [Chock] with my [written heart and slate-grey hair] [scrib-
>   bling blood] fringed rod and talking script
> [Chock-loud] in the   chimed the ground
>
> This minute's locked to learn me in the hour,
> Who sees it burn to break the scriptured cell
> And play the truant on the tip of days?

I, [said] rang the lock[s] at my temple, [but]
But [sentinel the] burn and break no [cap] marked boy, or
    beast, or taper

First vision that set fire to the air
In a [square] room [with] above the [final] town.

Fifty Two   "Shall gods be said to thump the clouds"
                                                August [1933]

The fourth stanza and the last stanza of the notebook poem were discarded
in the version published in *Twenty-five Poems* and *Collected*.

dye (l.14): Is "die" in the notebook; presumably "dye" is meant.

Fifty Three   "Matthias spat upon the lord"   16 August [1933]

Matthias (l. 1): A generic rather than specific Biblical character.
Reverend Crap (l. 3): Thomas wrote in the margin of the notebook, 'Rev David
Rees', the name of his mother's sister's husband, a clergyman in Swansea.
As part of his journeyman article-writing, Thomas had done a piece for the
Herald of Wales on 5 November 1932, a section of which was entitled 'End
of a Great Ministry', and was a straightforward eulogy: 'After the first Sunday
in November Mr Rees is to retire; an association that has lasted over a period
of nearly 35 years will be broken; and Mumbles, and indeed the whole of
Gower, will lose one of its best-known and best-loved inhabitants.' Apparently
the strain of writing this prose produced the reaction of a scathing poem. A
letter to Trevor Hughes of about this time shares some of the phraseology of
the poem and further indicates Thomas's mood as he comes to the end of this
notebook: 'Spitting on Christ prohibited. In the parks: Do not walk on God.
What shall it be? Jew's mucus or gentile's praise?' (*Letters* p. 161).

AUGUST 1933 NOTEBOOK

One   "The hand that signed the paper"   17 August 1933

Dedicated in the notebook to A.E.T. – Bert Trick, Thomas's Labour Party
friend.

These five blind kings . . . (ll. 17–20): This last stanza was crossed out thoroughly
in the notebook, and was dropped when the poem, otherwise unchanged,
was published in *New Verse* December 1935. The final version published in
Twenty-five Poems and *Collected* utilized the 'five kings' (l. 17) to replace the
original 'fingers' of l. 13.

Two   "Let for one moment a faith statement" 20 August 1933

Dedicated to T. H., Trevor Hughes, this poem was presumably written during Thomas's visit to his ex-Swansea friend's house on Perwell Ave., Rayners Lane, Harrow, Middlesex. Since Thomas wrote on the first page that the notebook was started on 23 August 1933, this poem, and "One" and "Three" also, were presumably copied in after his return to Swansea.

nightseed (l. 5): A made-up word for dreams.
maieutic (l. 13): Obstetric. Sleep is seen as the midwife of faith.

Three   "You are the ruler of this realm of flesh"
22 August 1933

Mahomet (l. 3): The hand is considered a Mahomet, or Mohammed, to whom the mountain (i.e. the body) comes.

Four   "That the sum sanity might add to nought"
24 August 1933

The opposite page of the notebook contains a draft of the first eight lines of the poem, not significantly different. The poem was rewritten, but not in the notebook. The version published in the *Swansea and West Wales Guardian* is included in the "Collateral Poems" section, below. It was at one point intended for *18 Poems*, but was not finally chosen for that volume, nor any other, by Thomas.

I would make genuflexion with the sheep (l. 12): The original line, before deletion, was 'I would reverse my collar to the sheep' (i.e. like a clergyman).
holla (l. 13): A fox-hunting cry, or holler.

Five   "Grief, thief of time, crawls off"   26 August 1933

The REVISION found on the opposite page of the notebook is practically the same as the first stanza of "Grief thief of time" as printed in *Twenty-five Poems* and *Collected*. According to Thomas's note, the revision was done at Glen Lough, Donegal, during his August 1935 stay in the west of Ireland, and was 'copied in later'. (The second stanza of the published "Grief thief of time" was supplied by poem "Eighteen" below.)

Six   "Shiloh's seed shall not be sown"   29 August 1933

By a salty dropsy sipping (l. 3): Thomas's asterisk at the end of this line and his footnote '*Southcott?' give some idea of what was on his mind in writing about miraculous birth. In 1814 the self-proclaimed prophetess Johanna Southcott, then sixty-four, declared she was to give birth to the promised saviour, Shiloh of Genesis 49:10. Possibly Thomas had read Blake's epigram,

'On the virginity of the Virgin and Johanna Southcott'. Nothing of this connection with Southcott is overtly preserved in the later version, much revised (no extant manuscript), published as "The seed-at-zero" in *Twenty-five Poems* and *Collected*.

Seven   "Before I knocked and flesh let enter"
6 September [1933]

On the page opposite in the notebook Thomas wrote:

> If God is praised in poem one
> Show no surprise when in the next
> I worship wood or sun or none:
> I'm hundred-heavened   rainbow sexed
>   and countless

– and drew an arrow pointing to "Before I knocked", indicating that the poem should be read with this thought in mind.

Thomas sent the poem to Pamela Hansford Johnson soon after it was written, and, comparing it with other poems he had sent her, said it contained 'more of what I consider to be of importance in my poetry' (*Letters* p. 39).

father (ll. 12 & 47): The typescript in the British Library capitalizes this word, stressing the divinity.

his ... him (ll. 48 & 54): Capitalized in the typescript.

his mother's womb (last line): In the typescript, this becomes: 'my mother's womb'.

My milk was curdled ... (ll. 25–30); *A virgin was* ... (ll. 49–52): The fifth and ninth stanzas were dropped from the poem as published in *18 Poems* and *Collected*.

Eight   "We see rise the secret wind behind the brain"
8 September [1933]

Thomas 'disagreed heartily' with Pamela Hansford Johnson that this poem should be included in *18 Poems* (*Letters* p. 125). It was not included, nor in any later volume.

Nine   "Take the needles and the knives"   12 September [1933]

A draft of the last four stanzas appears on the opposite page in the notebook, with no significant variant.

Sending the poem to Pamela Hansford Johnson in November 1933, Thomas wrote: 'For some reason I don't think you will like the needles and the knives. I don't think I do either, but there we are!' (*Letters* p. 23). In a note to this remark, Paul Ferris comments: 'On September 10, Dylan's father, D.J.

269

Thomas, had been admitted to hospital in London, to begin treatment with radium needles for cancer of the mouth, diagnosed two weeks earlier' (*Letters* p. 23).

sward (l. 42): Altered to 'wind' in the notebook.
die (l. 43): Altered to 'fall'.
And my father was the lord (l. 44): Deleted, and replaced by 'Like a wren through the trap land' – which was itself deleted without any replacement.

Ten   "Not forever shall the lord of the red hail"
15 September 1933

'To B.C.' – the dedicatee has not been identified. This is the first of several poems dated from Llangain, a village near Fernhill farm, where a family cottage, Blaen Cwm, was available to Thomas from time to time.

stamp (l. 6): Was 'morse' before alteration.
As fire falls . . . (ll. 7–12): A REVISION of this second stanza appears, unfinished, on the page opposite in the notebook.

> As fire falls, two hemispheres divide,
> Shall drown the boys of battle in their swill,
> The stock and steel that bayonet from the mud,
> The fields yet undivided behind the skull.
> Both mind and matter at the scalding word
> Shall drop their stuffs and scatter like a shell
> Your world and mine, one venom as they blew
>   hail

Thomas was at one point intending to revise the poem fully for inclusion in *18 Poems*, but that was not done (*Letters* p. 125).

Eleven   "Before we mothernaked fall"   16 September 1933

The version published in *New English Weekly* 30 July 1936 lacked the last four lines of the notebook poem, and added some punctuation to the rest. Thomas passed over this poem when compiling *Twenty-five Poems*, and did not subsequently reprint it.

build (l. 13): Was 'plumb' before alteration.
All is foreknown (last line): Deleted in the notebook.

Twelve   "The sun burns the morning"   16 September [1933]

Bethlehem (l. 10): Was deleted, and 'stable' interlined, which was itself in turn crossed out.
For the price of Christ . . . (ll. 14–15): These last two lines of the poem were crossed out in the notebook, and rewritten on the opposite page:

> A mother in labour pays twice her pain,
> Once for the Virgin's child, once for her own.

These revised lines appear in the typescript of the poem (Texas).

Thirteen   "My hero bares his nerves along my wrist"
17 September 1933

Turning (l. 17): Deleted in the notebook, and 'Praising' interlined.
Jack my father ... (ll. 21–26): This last stanza was crossed out in the notebook, and was omitted in *18 Poems* and *Collected*. It was adapted for use in poem "Eighteen" later in the notebook.

Fourteen – missing from the notebook.

Fifteen   "In the beginning was the three-pointed star"
18 September 1933

Thomas added a note 'See 40', referring to poem "Forty" later in the notebook, which is a revision of this early version and was published as "In the beginning" in *18 Poems* and *Collected*.

Joseph's grail (l. 11): Joseph of Arimathaea is said to have gathered into a chalice some of the blood of Christ at the crucifixion.
The star translated ... (ll. 22–24): These three lines were crossed out, and rewritten on the opposite page of the notebook:

> In the beginning was the three-tongue star
> Translating into light, that is all-tongued,
> The secret word spelling a single name.

Sixteen   "Love me, not as the dreamy nurses"
18 September 1933

This love poem was possibly written with Pamela Hansford Johnson in mind. Though they had not met, she had written him a fan letter early in September 1933 after his first appearance in the *Sunday Referee*. She had received this poem some time before the end of the year, for it is referred to as 'that love poem' in a letter of 25 December 1933 (*Letters* p. 80), just prior to its publication in the *Sunday Referee* of 7 January 1934. Thomas did not include it in any of his volumes.

dreamy (l. 1): An alternate word, 'midnight', was interlined in the notebook; but 'dreamy' was not crossed out. It appeared as 'dreaming' in the published version.

Seventeen   "For loss of blood I fell where stony hills"

25 September 1933

Thomas's note, 'In three Parts', was probably added, along with the part numbers, when this poem and the next two notebook poems were typed up together under the title "Jack of Christ". Glyn Jones was sent a copy of the typescript in 1934; it is now in the library of the University of Southern Illinois. The fourth and last stanzas were omitted in the typescript.

For loss of blood I fell (l. 1): Adapted for sonnet V of "Altarwise by owl-light" of *Twenty-five Poems* and *Collected*.
monster (l. 18): The typescript has 'frozen'.
hot-veined (l. 30): The typescript has 'raging'.

Eighteen   "Jack my father, let the knaves" 26 September 1933

Jack my father (ll. 1 & 5): The deleted last stanza of "My hero bares his nerves" (poem "Thirteen" above) provided this phrase and something of the theme. A REVISION is begun on the opposite page:

> Now Jack my fathers let the time-faced crook,
> Death flashing in his sleeve,
> With swag of bubbles in a bony sack
> Sneak down the century's grave,

These lines appear, with some changes, as the opening of the second stanza of the published poem "Grief thief of time" of *Twenty-five Poems* and *Collected*. (The first stanza was drawn from poem "Five" above.)

Nineteen   "The girl, unlacing, trusts her breast"

29 September 1933

manypointed light (l. 13): The typescript (Southern Illinois) has 'manypointed charms'.
Lorn (l. 23): Deleted in the notebook, but no alternative given.
needles' stroke (l. 38): Deleted, and 'surgeon wrist' interlined.
Jack (last line): Deleted, and 'the bride' interlined.

Twenty   "Through these lashed rings"   30 September 1933

In a typescript of this poem at Texas, Thomas did a REVISION of the second stanza in pencil in the margin:

> Through, I tell you, your two [cursing] midnight lips I pray
> To that unending sea around my island
> The water-spirit moves as it is bidden,

And with not one fear-beggared syllable
Praise him who springs and fills the tidal well.

The revision was not proceeded with, and the poem was not published by Thomas.

awkward (last line): Was 'ghostly', which was deleted, and 'tiny' interlined, which was in turn deleted, and 'awkward' interlined.

Twenty One   "Ape and ass both spit me forth" [October 1933]

The poem is incomplete as it stands; two notebook pages are missing.

Twenty Two   "The eye of sleep turned on me like a moon"
5 October 1933

Pamela Hansford Johnson must have praised this poem when she received it in October 1933, for Thomas replied: 'The "dream" poem that you like is *not* the best I have sent you. Only superficially is it the most visionary' (*Letters* p. 39). In a later letter, he considered the poem 'very bad indeed': 'I have rewritten "The Eye of Sleep" almost entirely, and it is now a little better, though still shaky on its rhythms and very woolly as to its intentions (if any)' (*Letters* p. 125). Thomas spelled out the rhyme scheme in another letter (*Letters* p. 40); the same consonantal rhyming is largely preserved in the revision (not extant in manuscript) which produced the "I fellowed sleep" of *18 Poems* and *Collected*.

wound his horn (l. 3): Pamela Hansford Johnson had apparently remembered this phrase as occurring in William Collins. Thomas countered: 'So the poor old snail has wound his horn before. It is a long time since I read the Ode to Evening, so long that my memory refuses all responsibility' (*Letters* p. 40).

furies (l. 34): Was deleted, and 'lights' interlined.

Twenty Three   "The force that through the green fuse"
12 October 1933

'To E.P.' – the dedicatee is not certainly identified. Paul Ferris in his biography *Dylan Thomas* suggested Evelyn Phillips, 'an attractive girl in the group that included Thomas'; but she told him that there is no special reason why the poem should have been dedicated to her (p. 327).

This poem convinced Victor Neuburg that the *Sunday Referee* should award Thomas the book prize, i.e. the publication of a first volume. In his review of the *Collected Poems* in the *New Statesman* on 15 May 1954, William Empson spoke of this event: 'What hit the town of London was the child Dylan publishing "The force that through the green fuse" as a prize poem in the *Sunday Referee*, and from that day he was a famous poet; I think the incident does some credit to the town, making it look less clumsy than you would think.'

Seven crossed out lines of a draft precede the poem in the notebook:

> The force that through the green fuse drives the flower
> Drives my green age; that blasts the roots of trees
> Is my destroyer.
> And I am dumb to tell the eaten rose
> How at my sheet goes the same crookèd worm,
> And dumb to holla thunder to the skies
> How at my cloths flies the same central storm.

the crookèd rose (l. 4): It is appropriate to think of Blake's "The Sick Rose". At the time of writing this poem of blighted youth Thomas thought himself very sick with tuberculosis. In a letter of around 5 November 1933 Thomas wrote to Pamela Hansford Johnson: 'A misanthropic doctor, who apparently did not like the way I did my eyebrows, has given me four years to live' (*Letters* p. 43).

How time has ticked a heaven round the stars (l. 20): This line had been: 'How time is all.' The version published in *Sunday Referee* 29 October 1933 had: 'And I am dumb to tell the timeless clouds/That time is all.' These lines were further amended before publication in *18 Poems* and *Collected*.

Twenty Four   "From love's first fever to her plague"
14 October 1933

The poem is completed as "Twenty Six", later in the notebook.

Twenty Five   "The almanac of time hangs in the brain"
16 October 1933

The syllables be said and said again (l. 14): Deleted in the notebook.

Twenty Six   "And from the first declension of the flesh"
17 October 1933

The root of tongues ends in a spentout cancer (l. 7): This may refer to Thomas's father, who had been in a London hospital the previous month having treatment for cancer of the mouth.

The soldered world debates (l. 28): This line was deleted in the notebook, and the last three lines of the poem were added in pencil. It is presumably about this ending that Thomas wrote to Pamela Hansford Johnson in November 1933: 'Your remark about the end of my Feverish poem is entirely justified. I plead guilty to bathos, but offer in excuse the fact that I copied out the poem as soon as I had written it, wanting to get it off to you and too hurried to worry about its conclusion. In the ordinary way I would never have passed it' (*Letters* p. 38). The whole of the last part of the notebook poem was left off for publication in *18 Poems* and *Collected*, where it was combined with poem

"Twenty Four" under the title "From love's first fever to her plague".

Twenty Seven "All that I owe the fellows of the grave"
[October 1933]

This poem, written in pencil on the left-hand pages, probably was a draft, waiting for a final adjustment before being entered on the right-hand blank pages. It did not, however, receive further attention.

Heir to the scalding veins that hold love's drop (l. 9): Found later use in "I dreamed my genesis" of *18 Poems* and *Collected*.

Twenty Eight "Here lie the beasts of man and here I feast"
25 October 1933

lie the beasts (l. 1): Was 'lie the worm' before alteration.
beast ... angels (l. 7): Was 'worm ... rose' before alteration. Thomas had written to Trevor Hughes that summer: 'Sometimes I want to go down to the cellar to be nearer the worms. Sometimes only a worm is companion, its grey voice at your ear the only voice' (*Letters* p. 19). His deletion of the word 'worm' twice in this poem might represent a move away from the cellar.

Twenty Nine "When once the twilight locks no longer"
11 November 1933

There was much revision of this poem (though not in any extant manuscript) before publication in *New Verse* June 1934, and further revision for *18 Poems* and *Collected*.

cancer (l. 17): 'I'm enclosing one poem, just finished. It's quite my usual stuff, I'm afraid, and quite probably you won't like it. But, honestly, the one "cancer" mentioned *is* necessary' – Thomas to Pamela Hansford Johnson, November 1933 (*Letters* p. 57).
emerods (l. 40): Biblical spelling of 'hemorrhoids'.

Thirty "Light breaks where no sun shines"
20 November 1933

A draft of the first few lines preceded the poem on the opposite page in the notebook. The poem was published without revision in the *Listener* 14 March 1934, in *18 Poems* and *Collected*.

Thirty One "I fellowed sleep who kissed between the brains"
27 November 1933

The first line and a few other phrases from this notebook poem were grafted on to poem "Twenty Two" ("The eye of sleep"), earlier in the notebook, to produce the "I fellowed sleep" of *18 Poems* and *Collected*. (No manuscript of the revision process is extant.)

And worlds hang on the trees (last line): Became the last line of the revised, published "When once the twilight locks" of *18 Poems* and *Collected*.

Thirty Two   "See, says the lime, my wicked milks"
13 December 1933

Thomas's pencilled note in the margin, 'See 28', may refer to poem "Twenty Eight" earlier in the notebook, "Here lie the beasts of man", with which it shares mortuary imagery, including the image of 'milk' as the fluid of the grave. Thomas wrote to Pamela Hansford Johnson soon after completing this poem:

> A new poem accompanies this. I suppose it's my usual stuff again, and even a little more death-struck. But don't be put off by my anatomical imagery, which I explained months ago. Because I so often write in terms of the body, of the death, disease, and breaking of the body, it doesn't necessarily mean that my Muse (*not* one of my favourite words) is a sadist. For the time at least, I believe in the writing of poetry from the flesh, and, generally, from the dead flesh. So many modern poets take the *living* flesh as their object, and, by their clever dissecting, turn it into a carcase. I prefer to take the *dead* flesh, and, by any positivity of faith and belief that is in me, build up a *living* flesh from it (*Letters* pp. 72–73).

Thirty Three   "This bread I break was once the oat"
24 December 1933

My wine you drink, my bread you break (last line): A draft of the poem was done on the opposite page, which differs only in this last line, which was: 'God's bread you break, you drain His cup.' The religious emphasis of this Christmas poem was further increased by the title given to the draft, "Breakfast Before Execution". There was a one word change in this last line – 'break' became 'snap' – before publication in *New English Weekly* on 16 July 1936, which version was reprinted in *Twenty-five Poems* and *Collected*, with one notorious misprint, 'wind' instead of 'wine' in l. 6, corrected in later editions of the *Collected Poems*.

Thirty Four   "Your pain shall be a music in your string"
12 January 1934

Twixt (l. 12): Deleted in the notebook, but not replaced by anything else.

Thirty Five   "A process in the weather of the heart"
2 February 1934

womb (l. 8): Was originally 'tomb'; the 't' was crossed out, and 'w' interlined –

a rather graphic illustration of the interchangeability of two such words in this kind of process poem.

unangled (l. 12): In a draft of the poem on the opposite page in the notebook, the variant here (the only notable variant) was 'unplumbed'. This indicates that 'unangled' means 'not fished with rod and line'. Without further revision, the notebook poem was published in the *Sunday Referee* on 11 February 1934, and in *18 Poems* and *Collected*.

Thirty Six   "Foster the light, nor veil the bushy sun"
23 February 1934

For a revised version, as published in the *Sunday Referee* 28 October 1934, see the "Collateral Poems" section of the present volume. There was further revision (no manuscript extant) to produce the version published in *18 Poems* and *Collected*.

Foster the light (l. 1): According to Trevor Hughes, Thomas took the opening phrase of this poem from a letter Hughes had sent him on hearing about Thomas's father's illness in January 1934, and which had contained the sentence: 'Foster the light, and God be with you' (typescript in Buffalo Library).

Thirty Seven   "The shades of girls all flavoured"   March 1934

Our eunuch dreams (l. 11): When the poem came to be revised for publication in *New Verse* April 1934, the revised poem began with this line. Lines 1–10 of the notebook poem were dropped, but certain phrases utilized in the revision.

Groom the dark brides ... (ll. 15–16): The original lines, written tentatively in pencil and then deleted, were: 'Go groom the brides and kiss the salt shades sweet/As the bees' creams.' The present lines were interlined.

When love, awoken, hungers in her womb (l. 20): This was interlined over the original line, deleted: 'When, sad of gut, love sacks her dream.' *New Verse* had a variant line: 'When love awakes her delver to the worm.'

The sunny gentlemen, the Welshing rich (part III, l. 5): This was interlined over a deleted line: 'The sunny gents who piddle in the porch'.

This is the world. Have faith. (part III, l. 16): The poem at first ended with this line. A four line stanza followed 'Or drive the night-geared forth' (part III, l. 6).

> Which is the dream, and which the photograph?
> And which is life, is death?
> This is the world which whispers in our breath:
> This is the world. Have faith.
>> *March '34*

This stanza was deleted, and replaced by the four lines beginning 'The photograph is married'. The poem was completed a few pages later in the notebook. After Geoffrey Grigson of *New Verse* had had the poem for some time, Thomas wrote to him:

> I have been reading over again my poem starting 'Our eunuch dreams ...', and am struck more forcibly than before by what might seem to be the jarring optimism of the first six lines of the fourth part. I suggest that this revised stanza sounds far less false:

> > This is the world: the lying likeness of
> > Our strips of stuff that tatter as we move
> > Loving from rag to bone;
> > The dream that kicks the buried from their sack
> > And lets their trash be honoured as the quick.
> > Suffer this world to spin.

> But, of course, it's entirely in your hands. If you think this revised version to be better in any way, I do hope you'll use it (*Letters* p. 106).

However, Grigson did not alter the version first sent to him. Thus, the original notebook wording appears in *New Verse*, and *18 Poems* and *Collected*.

Thirty Eight   "Where once the waters of your face"

18 March 1934

course (l. 11): Became 'source' in a typescript (Southern Illinois), and was published as such in the *Sunday Referee* on 25 March 1934, and in *18 Poems* and *Collected*.

Sage (l. 21): Became 'Grim' in the typescript, but was published as here.

Thirty Nine   "I see the boys of summer in their ruin"

April 1934

Thomas told Pamela Hansford Johnson in a letter of 2 May 1934 that this poem would open his first book (*Letters* p. 125); he did not change that opinion.

barren (l. 2): Was 'low' in a first draft on the opposite page of the notebook.

Of love and light (l. 23): Became 'Of doubt and dark' in *New Verse* April 1934. (Geoffrey Grigson has said, in conversation, that he as editor did not change the manuscript submitted by Thomas.) The notebook reading was restored for *18 Poems* and *Collected*.

Oh (l. 24): The 'Oh' is written over a previous 'I' in the notebook. For *18 Poems* the 'Oh' throughout was changed to 'O'.

Forty   "In the beginning was the three-pointed star"

April 1934

A note by Thomas, 'See Fifteen', refers to the poem "Fifteen" earlier in this notebook, which was a first version. After some changes to the last two lines, this later version was published as "In the beginning" in *18 Poems* and *Collected*.

spread (l. 4): This word was deleted, and 'forked' interlined.

Forty One   "If I was tickled by the rub of love"   30 April 1934

Thomas sent this poem to Pamela Hansford Johnson on 2 May 1934: 'The poem is, I think, the best I've written – I've said that to you about a lot of mine, including all sorts of wormy beasts. It may be obscure, I don't know, but it honestly was not meant to be' (*Letters* p. 126).

was (ll. 1, 10, 18, 22): Appeared as 'was' in *New Verse* August 1934, but was corrected to 'were' for *18 Poems* and *Collected*.
Chalking the jakes with green things of the brain (l. 16): This line was altered interlinearly to become: 'Chalking the walls with green girls their men.'
old age upon (l. 24): Altered to 'old manhood on'.
The biting days ... (ll. 27–28): These two lines were altered to read: 'The sea of scums could drown me as it broke/Dead on the sweetheart's toes.'
bud that forks ... herrings smelling in the sea (ll. 31 and 33): These phrases were taken from the original stanza three of the poem:

> If from the first some mother of the wind
> Gave suck to such a bud as forks my eye,
> I would not fear the howling round the cots
> As time on time the lean searibbons round
> Parched shires in dry lands, and the rat's lot,
> Nor all the herring smelling of the sea
> Nor the death in the light.

This stanza had been derived from poem "Twenty Seven" in the *February 1933 Notebook*, "Pass through twelve stages". It was thoroughly crossed out in the notebook, and not used in the published version.

COLLATERAL POEMS

(1) "I have not moulded this marble"   [1930]

This poem exists in manuscript, in Thomas's hand, at the Humanities Research Center, Texas. It is similar to other poems written in 1930, and is probably a draft that would normally have been entered into a notebook, with or without revision. After l. 2 in the manuscript are two thoroughly deleted lines that seem remote from the mood of the rest of the poem, and are omitted here. They are, however, interesting in themselves:

> My spirit has feasted with the dead,
> And now the hospital takes me in hand.

(2) "Calling temerity to see"   [April 1931]

This is the second of two poems written by Thomas in the fly-leaf of his copy of Osbert Sitwell's *Argonauts* (1927), now in the Humanities Research Center, Texas. The first of the two is a draft, dated 29 April 1931, that, with minor revision, became poem "XLVIII" of the *1930–1932 Notebook*, "Sever from what I trust". The present poem was left unrevised, and does not appear in any extant notebook.

(3) "You too have seen the sun a bird of fire"   [April 1932]

Entitled "Youth Calls to Age" when published in *Herald of Wales* on 23 April 1932, this poem has no manuscript source. It is by no means certain that it was written as a tribute to any particular forerunner, but it was adapted to that end, appearing with an article Thomas wrote on "Verse of James Chapman Woods – Swansea's Greatest Poet – a Critical Estimate". There is nothing in the article to suggest that James Chapman Woods had 'seen the sun a bird on fire', as the poem has it.

(4) "That sanity be kept I sit at open windows"
                                                          [August 1933]

This could likely have been the missing poem "Forty Nine", torn out of the *February 1933 Notebook*. It was published with the title "That Sanity Be Kept" in the *Sunday Referee*, 3 September 1933. Pamela Hansford Johnson wrote to Thomas about it; he replied in a letter of 15 September 1933: 'The more I think of my Referee poem the less I like it. The idea of myself, sitting in the open window, in my shirt, and imagining myself as some Jehovah of the West, is really odd. If I were some Apollo it would be different. As a matter of fact, I am a little person with much untidy hair' (*Letters* p. 22).

(5) "That the sum sanity might add to nought"   [May 1934]

In a letter of 2 May 1934 Thomas referred to ' "That The Sum Sanity" (revised)' as one of the poems to be included in *18 Poems*. This revision of poem "Four" of the *August 1933 Notebook* was published in the *Swansea and West Wales Guardian* on 8 June 1934 (entitled "Twelve" – from its number in a sequence of typed poems); but it was not chosen for reprinting in a volume.

(6) "Do you not father me"   [September 1934]

This is an early version of the "Do you not father me" published in *Twenty-five Poems* and *Collected*. It exists in a typescript among the Pamela Hansford Johnson papers at Buffalo along with a typescript of "Especially when the October wind"; it may, as that poem was, be a revision of an early version of the 1932 period. But no manuscript exists. As typed, it probably belongs to around September 1934, when *18 Poems* was being prepared. Of the two typescripts, "Especially when the October wind" was chosen at the last minute for *18 Poems*; "Do you not father me" was not. It was revised again in the summer of 1935, and first published in *The Scottish Bookman*, October 1935.

(7) "Foster the light, nor veil the feeling moon"
[October 1934]

On about 23 October 1934 Thomas wrote to Pamela Hansford Johnson: 'I have, of course, in the weakness of my spirit, sent some clumsy poem for the Referee' (*Letters* p. 169). He had sent a somewhat revised version of poem "Thirty Six" of the *August 1933 Notebook*, which was published in the *Sunday Referee* the following Sunday, 28 October 1934. The present text comes from that publication with several misprints corrected. This version was revised extensively for publication in *Contemporary Poetry and Prose*, May 1936, reprinted in *Twenty-five Poems* and *Collected*.

(8) "First I knew the lamb on knocking knees"   [1934]

This poem in typescript in the British Library is a rewriting of poem "Twenty Eight" in the *February 1933 Notebook*. It is undated, but presumably was done in 1934 when Thomas was thinking in terms of tighter, rhymed poems. During the summer of 1935, he used phrases from the notebook poem in sonnet III of "Altarwise by owl-light" of *Twenty-five Poems* and *Collected*.

(9) "Your breath was shed"   [1934, 1944]

The early version, "Thy Breath Was Shed", was sent to Pamela Hansford Johnson at least by April 1934; it is included in her 'abortive list of poems' proposed for Thomas's first volume. In a letter of 2 May 1934, he calls this poem and others of her list 'very bad indeed' (*Letters* p. 125). He did not therefore include this early version in *18 Poems*, nor did he publish it elsewhere. There is no extant manuscript; so we rely on Pamela Hansford

Johnson's memory of it, as far as it goes. She remembers it as having, at one time, the title "The Candle", and beginning:

> Thy breath was shed
> Invisible to weave
> Around my carven head
> A carven eve.

The later version was not published until *Poetry* (*London*) No. 9 (1944), which is the source of the present text.

Index of Titles and First Lines

Titles of poems in italics.

Where the first line of a poem is exactly the same as the title, it is not repeated.